CW00566617

MANSFIELD
THROUGH TIME
Gerry van Tonder

AMBERLEY

I dedicate this publication to Dr Andries van Tonder and Dr Ashleigh van Tonder, my two children, of whom I am extremely proud.

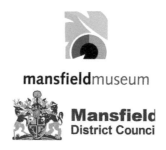

mansfieldmuseum

Mansfield
District Counci

I acknowledge, with profound gratitude, the unreserved and invaluable assistance received from Mansfield Museum curator Liz Weston MBE, and member of staff Charlotte Morgan, whom Liz assigned to me to help find images from the museum's archives.

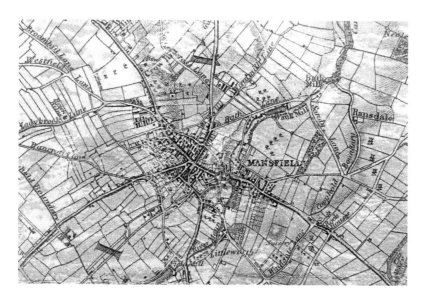

George Sanderson's map of Mansfield (1835).

First published 2016

Amberley Publishing
The Hill, Stroud, Gloucestershire, GL5 4EP
www.amberley-books.com

Copyright © Gerry van Tonder, 2016

The right of Gerry van Tonder to be identified as the Author of this work has been asserted in accordance with the Copyrights, Designs and Patents Act 1988.

ISBN 978 1 4456 5957 2 (print)
ISBN 978 1 4456 5958 9 (ebook)

All rights reserved. No part of this book may be reprinted or reproduced or utilised in any form or by any electronic, mechanical or other means, now known or hereafter invented, including photocopying and recording, or in any information storage or retrieval system, without the permission in writing from the Publishers.

British Library Cataloguing in Publication Data.
A catalogue record for this book is available from the British Library.

Printed in Great Britain.

Acknowledgements

I wish to extend my sincere gratitude to the friendly and helpful people of Mansfield. Wherever I went, pedestrians showed a genuine interest in what I was doing.

When 'cold-calling' at the fire station and the central police station, the willingness to assist was tangible. Special thanks to Firefighter Malc Ridge and Constable Paul Hughes for their help during my photo shoots at their respective places of work.

Thank you for the ongoing support to Nick Tomlinson and his team at Picture the Past, the not-for-profit project that started in 2002 and aims to make historic images from the library and museum collections across the whole of Derby, Derbyshire, Nottingham and Nottinghamshire, available via a completely free-to-use website. I am pleased to say that we have established a valuable reciprocal relationship aimed at furthering the preservation of the history of Derbyshire and Nottinghamshire.

Much of the historical and anecdotal content in this publication has been gleaned from contemporary editions of the *Nottingham Evening Post* and *Nottinghamshire Guardian*.

All the photos that do not carry a credit are those of the author.

Introduction

A river in name only (as most will argue), the Maun surreptitiously and quietly wends its way through Mansfield from the west. Vast tracts of its progress go unseen as it disappears from view under man-made structures and, therefore, largely unheeded as the *raison d'être* for the very existence of this west Nottinghamshire town.

A derivative of the Celtic word *Mamm* for 'Mother Goddess', the Maun and its surrounds provided adequate resources to sustain durable habitation and sustenance agriculture.

At the time of the Norman invasion, the king owned a manor in the area, of which Mansfield was a part, most likely as a base for necessary administrative functions in the northern reaches of the county.

Growth over the ensuing centuries was at a typically rural pace. Textile weaving and small-business stone quarrying developed, thanks in some part to the transport routes that passed through the village, sited where it was on the western fringes of Sherwood Forest.

In 1227, the settlement was granted a royal market charter, indicating that an agrarian cash economy had developed. Schools and places of worship sprang up in response to the demands of a quintessential expanding and evolving English village.

Following the invention of the stocking frame in the late sixteenth century, knitting frames became popular in Mansfield, numbering several hundred by the end of the eighteenth century. Hops malting also gave rise to the embryonic stages of beer brewing.

During this period of growth, Cromford-born entrepreneur Richard Arkwright introduced the world to factory-scale production of spun cotton cloth. He harnessed the cheap waterpower

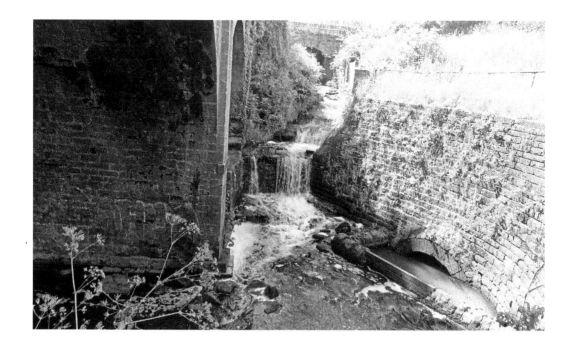

of the River Derwent to drive his machines and fuel his radical foresight – the Industrial Revolution was born. Within years, hydropower from the Maun spawned a series of prosperous mills along its course. The town's population reached 6,000.

This industrialisation momentum gathered pace in the 1800s, underpinned by the arrival of the railway in 1819. Over the next fifty years, lines opened to termini in the Erewash Valley and Nottingham, and in true, grand Brunel fashion of the period, a railway viaduct was erected across Mansfield, followed in 1872 with the opening of the Midland Railway Station.

With the development of steam power, it was inevitable that the small River Maun could no longer cope with the demand for industrial power, which now also included several foundries. In 1902, the Sherwood Colliery shaft was sunk, followed two years later by the recently formed Bolsover Colliery Co., who commenced sinking a shaft at the Mansfield Colliery near Crown Farm. The pit would last eighty-three years before viability and safety concerns brought the pithead wheels to a final standstill.

Arguably however, these were the halcyon days that fuelled new suburban conurbations, replete with schools, health facilities, shops and churches. Forest Town provides a perfect example of a settlement that owes its very existence to coal and the mining jobs that sustained a living community.

A succession of progressive, independently minded town councils always appeared fully cognisant of their burghers' welfare through recreation. Swimming baths opened in 1904; Titchfield Park was presented to the town by the 6th Duke of Portland soon after; and, in 1931, the Nottinghamshire Playing Fields spent £9,000 on converting '28 acres of wasteland covered by gorse', and known as the Racecourse, into a 'magnificent' recreation ground.

The Edwardian era introduced Mansfield's first theatres and picture houses, but by the 1920s, the mills started closing and some were demolished.

Mansfield's economy continued to diversify, however. Metal Box acquired Barringer, Wallis and Manners and, in doing so, secured the manufacture of specialised packaging in the town

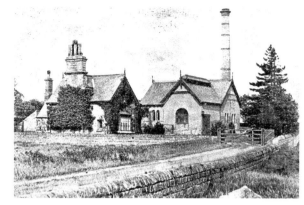

The steam-driven water-pumping station Gregory's Quarry, Nottingham Road (built in 1870).

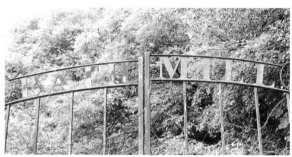

right to this day. The manufacturing of boots and shoes, started by Royce & Gascoigne in Mansfield in 1867, went on to develop a range of quality ladies' shoes by the Mansfield Shoe Co. – the group only stopped production in 2004.

In quick succession, and following what was described by the BBC in 1984 as 'the most bitter industrial dispute in British history', Mansfield's coal pits closed. The twin, multi-wheeled pitheads on Clipstone Road, towering and silent, serve as monuments to the men and women who *were* Mansfield coal.

In November 1891, the then Duke of Portland presented the borough of Mansfield with the Birmingham-made mayoral chain to commemorate the 'higher dignity of incorporation' conferred upon the town. Mr G. H. Hibbert became the first incumbent to wear this symbol of high civic office.

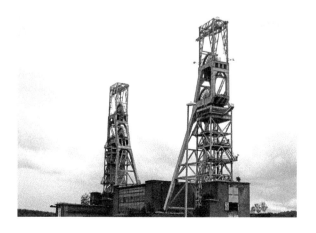

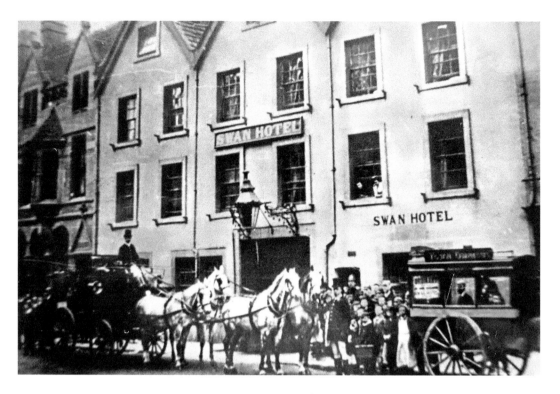

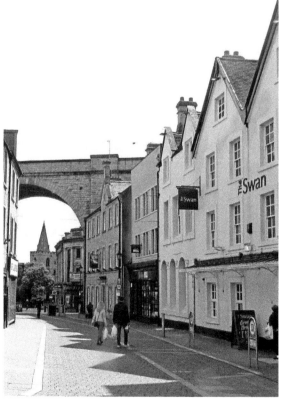

The Swan

With the staff resplendent in top hats, a magnificent coach and four greys calls at the Swan Hotel in this image from the second half of the nineteenth century. Centrally situated on Church Street, just off Mansfield's Market Place, this coaching inn had been an important revictualling stop on regional routes since the 1700s. The arrival of the railway would see the gradual demise of such inns, with the last mail service operating the Chesterfield leg early in 1856. Now a pub, The Swan sits in the shadow of the rail viaduct. (*Above*: Courtesy of Mansfield Museum)

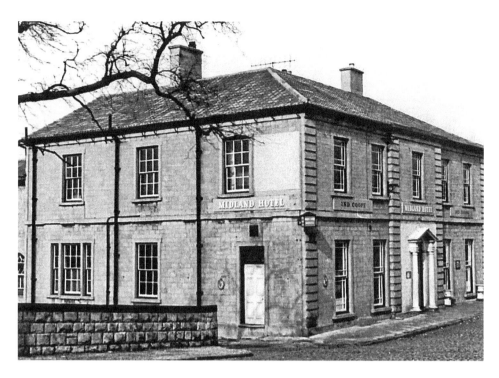

The Midland Hotel

Within a few minutes' walking distance from the train station, this late-Georgian hotel, with a commanding view over the town, has retained the sash windows typical of the period. Formerly known as Broom House, the building became a hotel in around 1820. Years later, the hotel yard provided a popular venue of auctions in execution of property. The hotel stables were also the home of the Mansfield Horse and Carriage Repository, from where horses were auctioned for 2s 6d a head. Today, the family-run hotel also offers conference facilities. (*Above*: Courtesy of Mansfield Museum)

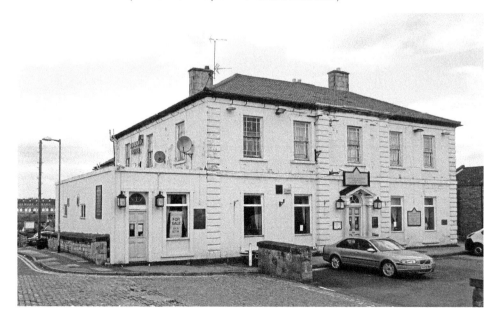

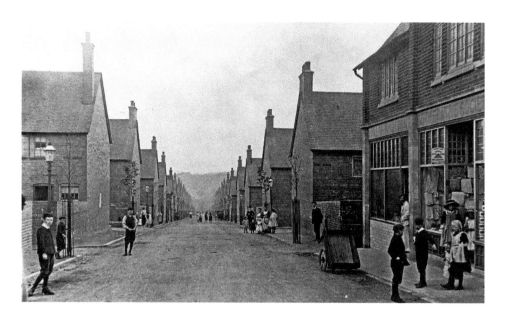

The Avenues, Forest Town

In 1904, a colliery shaft was sunk near the eponymous Crown Farm, resulting in a rapidly growing Forest Town community springing up to meet the sudden demand for worker housing and amenities. A grid of high-density dwellings was the first to be erected, and, uninspiringly, christened The Avenues. The contemporary image below reveals unchanged homes except for telephone cables and TV aerials now adorning the original regimented rows of buildings. (*Above*: Courtesy of Mansfield Museum)

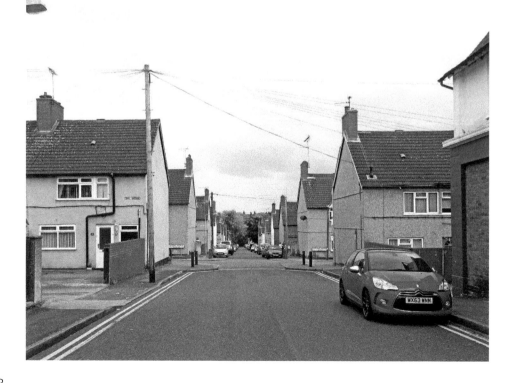

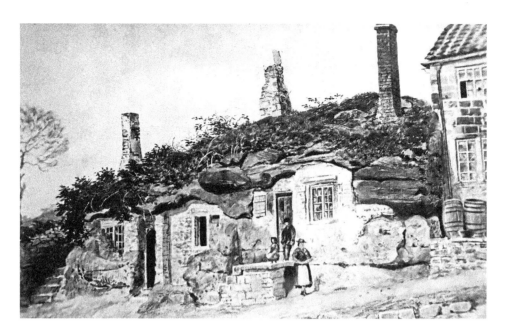

Rock Houses

Mansfield artist Albert Sorby Buxton imbues, in his painting above, a rustic charm in these ancient cave dwellings on Rock Hill. The turn-of-the-nineteenth-century picture shows hillside hollows into which, in the words of the late-Victorian historian W. H. Groves, [homes] were made by squatters who saw an easy means of escaping rent and possessing comfortable apartments into the bargain'. Ground subsidence eventually made the caves uninhabitable. In 1980, the council secured the site, which is rapidly becoming overgrown today. (*Above*: Courtesy of Mansfield Museum)

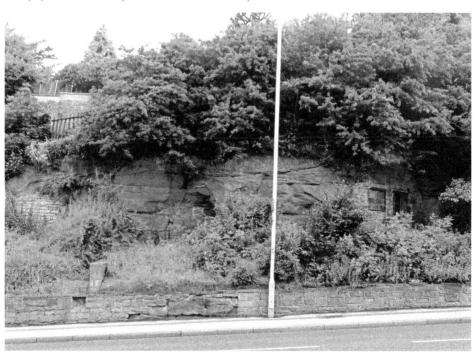

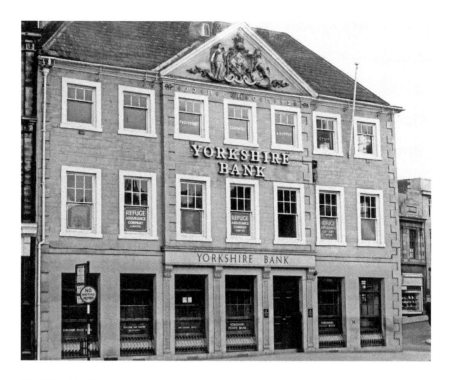

The Moot Hall

Funded by English noblewoman Henrietta Harley (née Holles), Countess of Oxford and Countess Mortimer, the hall was erected in the Market Place in 1752. The colourful Oxford coat of arms adorns the pediment tympanum facing the market square. At the time, the hall's utilitarian function was that of a venue at which town folk would meet to discuss community issues. The Yorkshire Bank assumed occupancy in 1921. It was granted Grade II-listed status in 1955 and ground-floor rooms are now occupied by the Nationwide Building Society. (*Above*: Courtesy of Mansfield Museum)

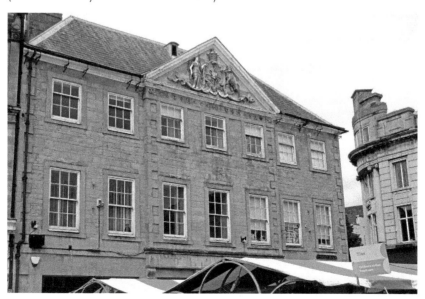

Leckenby's

The trade name of Crow & Leckenby was synonymous with the selling of quality coffee which, in February 1913, it advertised at 5s 6d for 3lbs. Today, many remember walking into the family departmental store in Leeming Street, with their senses assailed by the fragrant aroma of freshly ground coffee. Pasikonik (meaning 'grasshopper') is the current tenant: a Polish grocery shop that reflects the contemporary cultural diversity of Mansfield. (*Right*: Courtesy of Mansfield Museum)

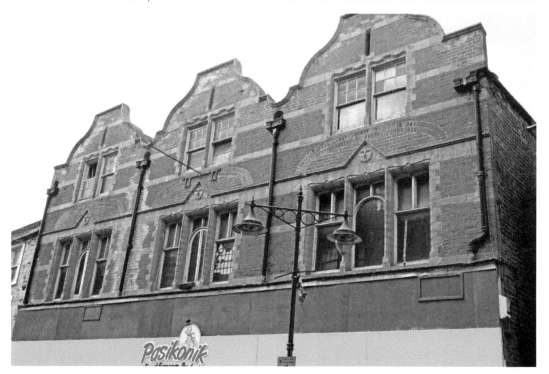

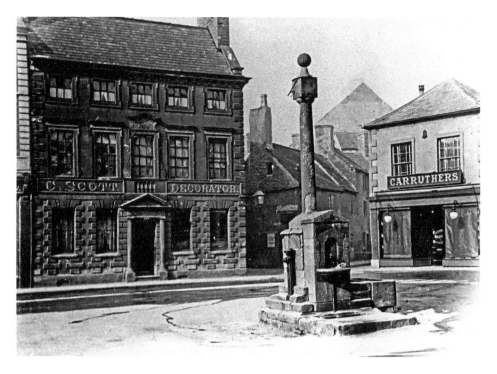

Waverley House

Constructed in West Gate in 1754 with surplus ashlar and coursed squared stone from the Moot Hall, the three-storey building features a classical entrance with a pediment supported by Doric columns. Standing over the former cattle market, the former residential property has for many years been occupied by local solicitors Buxton Hopkins. (*Above*: Courtesy of Mansfield Museum)

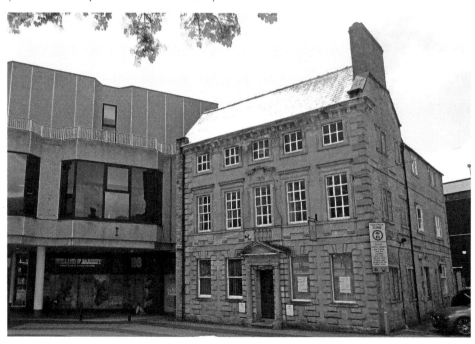

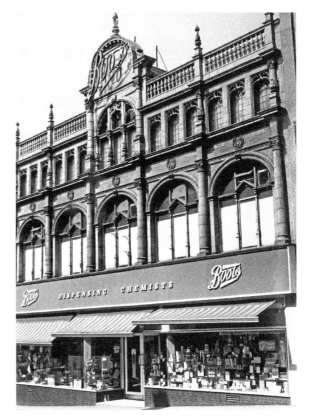

The Boots Building

Built at the turn of the twentieth century for the Nottingham-based cash chemist Boots, this listed building in Leeming Street presents an eclectic façade of Renaissance Revival and decorated Gothic, the latter evidenced by the tracery atop the upper-floor windows. The ground-floor shopfronts – now boarded up – are a much later addition to facilitate street-level merchandising. The metal 'Boots' sign no longer graces the semicircular gable above the hidden roof; the building stands empty, its grand appearance tarnished by more recent signage. (*Above*: Courtesy of Mansfield Museum)

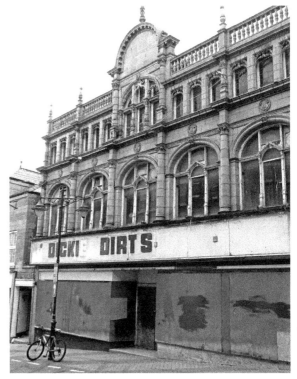

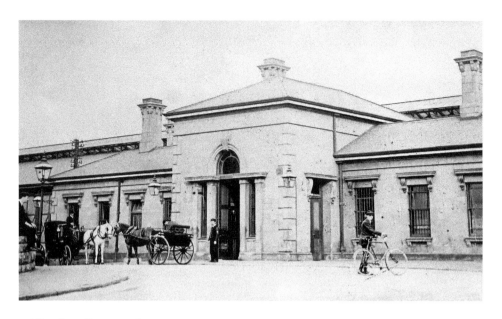

Midlands Railway Station

Opened on 2 March 1872, and situated on the newly laid Robin Hood line, the Mansfield rail terminus was originally established by the Mansfield & Pinxton Railway to freight coal from collieries in Pinxton and the Erewash Valley. Rail wagons were originally horse-drawn. Having changed very little over time, the station was closed in 1964, only to be refurbished and reopened thirty-one years later. (*Above*: Courtesy of Mansfield Museum)

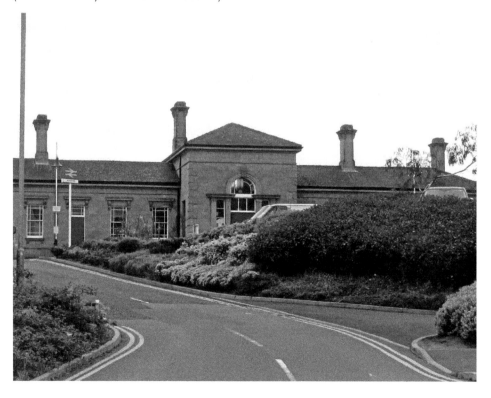

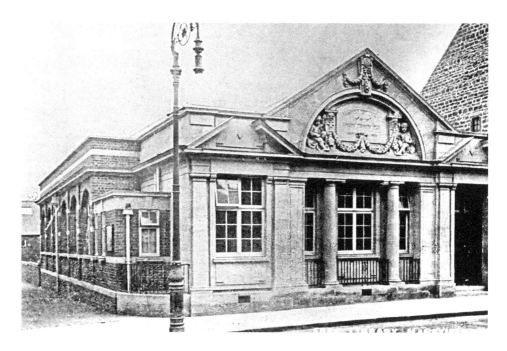

The Old Library

On 24 May 1905, the *Nottingham Evening Post* reported on a 'handsome new library, which Mr Andrew Carnegie has generously presented to Mansfield, and which has been erected in a site on Leeming Street, given by the Duke of Portland', which would be opened the following day by Mayor G. H. Hibbert. Designed by Mr E. R. Sutton of Nottingham in the baroque revival style, the Mansfield Arts Centre now occupies the building. (*Above*: Courtesy of Mr D. Bradbury www.picturethepast.org.uk)

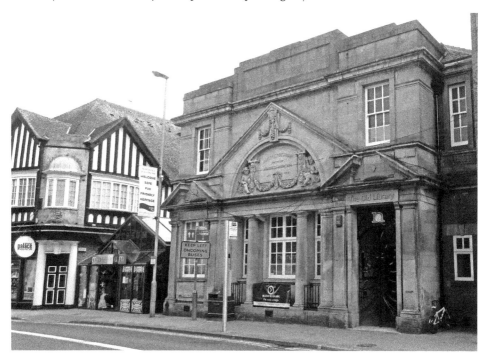

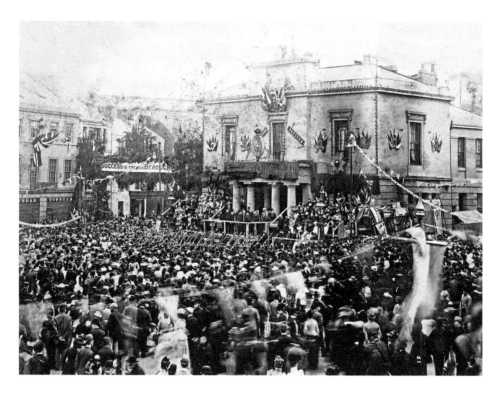

Town Hall

A momentous day in Mansfield's civic history is celebrated on the steps of the town hall at the public reading of the incorporation into a borough charter on 14 July 1891. Businesses closed their doors as a holiday spirit gripped the thousands gathered in the Market Place where, with a royal salute fired by the Mansfield Co. of Volunteers, the town 'attained the dignity of a borough'. In the contemporary image below, the former town hall, now providing office space, remains a focal point of the town's pride. (*Above*: Courtesy of Mansfield Museum)

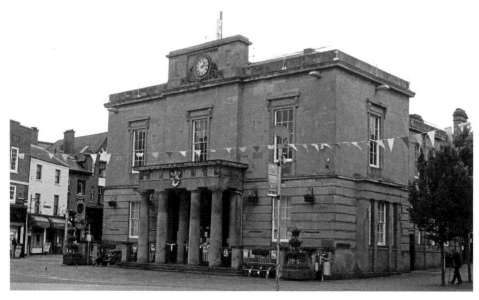

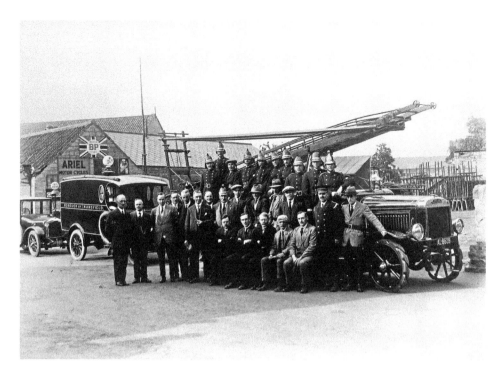

A Fire Service

A magnificent, well-polished, pre-1930s Leyland fire engine, complete with firemen and town dignitaries and support van, captures the very essence of a bygone era in the public service of the borough. In the photo below, Mansfield firefighter Malc Ridge proudly stands by today's state-of-the-art Scania P270 Browns Rescue Pump outside the brigade's station on Rosemary Street. (*Above*: Courtesy of Mansfield Museum)

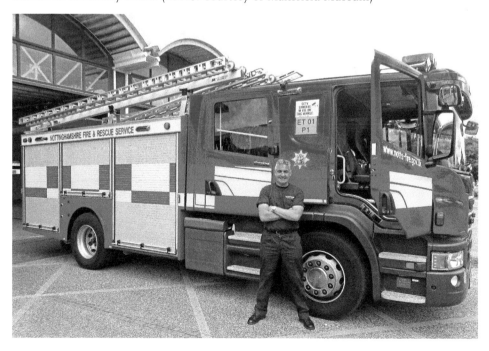

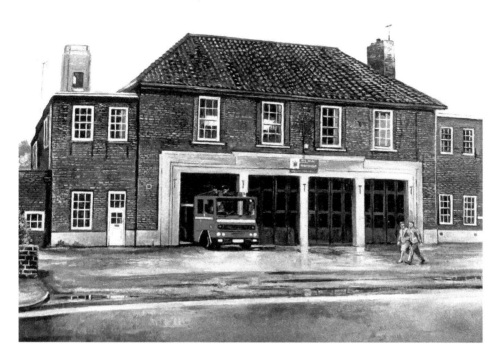

Fire Station

Built in 1939, the old fire station, depicted in the Dennis Barron painting above, replaced the facility on Toothill Lane. The work was commissioned around 1999 to commemorate the opening of the fire station. In July 1997, the building was demolished to make way for the new station on the same site on Rosemary Street. The original tower survives; it was once the home of the town's Second World War air-raid siren. (*Below*: Taken by author, courtesy of Mansfield Fire Station)

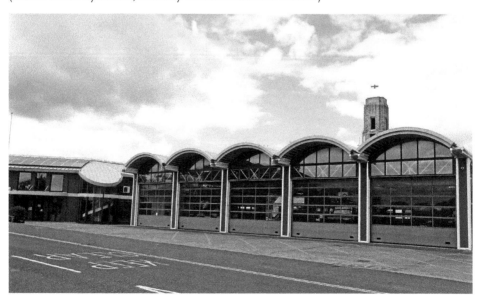

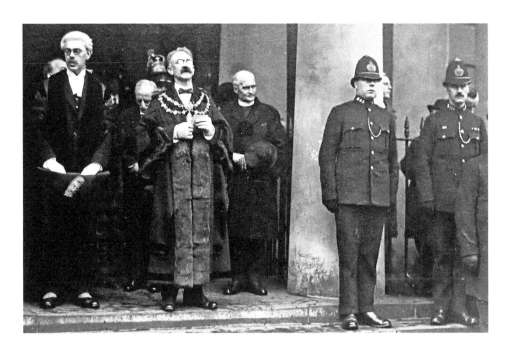

A Town Bobby

A Mansfield constable stands smartly to attention while Mayor D. H. Maltby inaugurates the celebration for the anniversaries of the market charter which was granted to the town in 1227, and the July Fair charter in 1377. Guarding the civic and community leaders at the entrance to the town hall, the policeman's stiff uniform, with whistle chain and glossy footwear, is in sharp contrast with Mansfield's 2754 Constable Paul Hughes's telescopic 'truncheon' and protective stab vest. (*Above*: Courtesy of Mansfield Museum)

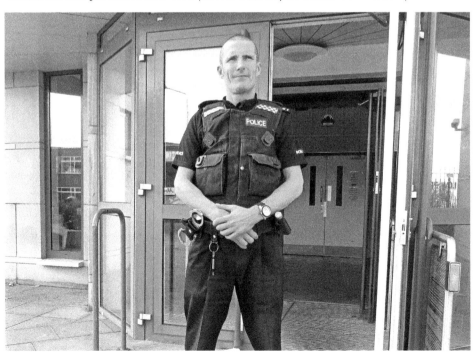

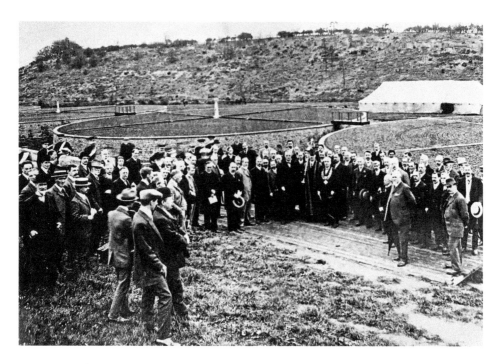

Sewage Works

Councillors and town folk witness the Duke of Portland opening the new £40,000 sewage works on a site lying between Bath Lane and the Sheepwash. Prior to this event on 10 May 1912, discharging sewage into the River Maun had been regarded as 'sufficient'. With an estimated population at the time of 40, 000, the purification facility continued to expand with time along the western bank of the river, now almost totally hidden from sight within a heavily wooded area. (*Above*: Courtesy of Mansfield Museum)

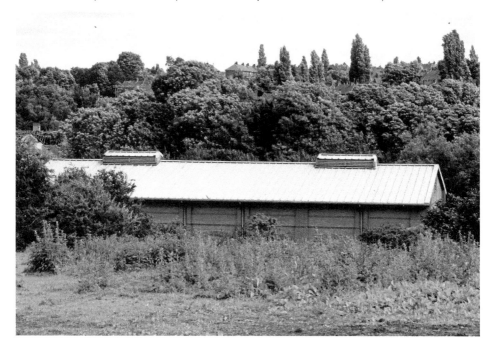

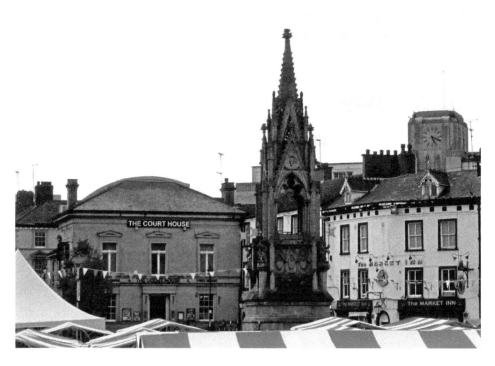

Court House

Dating back to 1840, the sombre countenance of the former probate office, savings bank and courthouse almost belies the current usage – that of public house. The foundation stone for a new magistrates' court on Rosemary Street (*pictured below*) was laid in September 1994 by the chairman, Mr Peter Burgess, and Mr George Fish of the Nottinghamshire County Council and Nottinghamshire Magistrates' Court Committee, respectively. Opened by the Princess Royal two years later, the court addresses legal issues which include high court, crime, divorce, domestic violence, housing possession and money claims. (*Above*: Courtesy of Mansfield Museum)

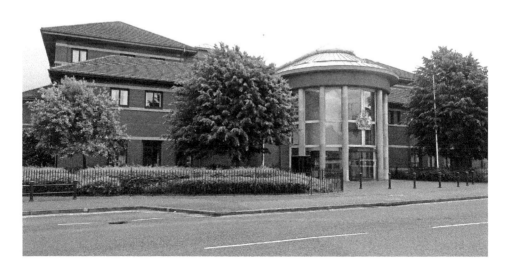

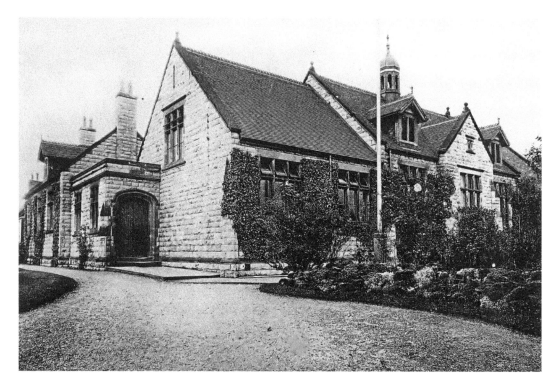

Brunts Technical School

On 31 July 1894, Lord Belper ceremoniously used a gold key to open Mansfield's new school on Woodhouse Road. In 1709, property owner Samuel Brunts – 'a gentleman of Mansfield' – had bequeathed £4 a year from his charity estate for the education of poor boys in the town. Today, the custodians of Brunts' legacy, now a business centre, guarantee the future of this fine stone building. The only visible change is the missing steeple, which was removed at some point in time. (*Above*: Courtesy of Mansfield Museum)

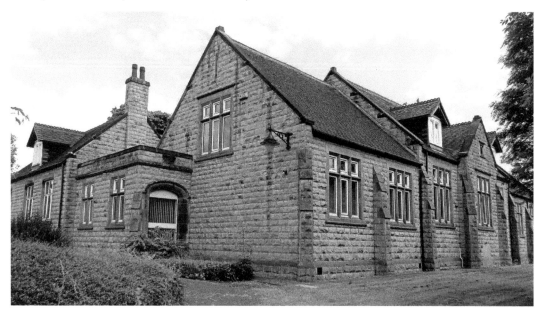

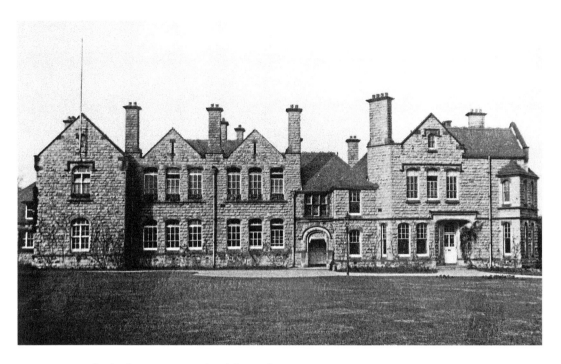

Queen Elizabeth Grammar School for Girls

Hidden from view behind large trees and an ancient wall on Woodhouse Road, and now residential apartments (*pictured below*) is this grand 1891, ashlar-dressed, former grammar school for girls. A beneficiary of the Brunt's Charity, the Osborne-Smith-designed building was vacated in 1993 when the school merged with the Queen Elizabeth Grammar School for Boys on Chesterfield Road. (*Above*: Courtesy of Mansfield Museum)

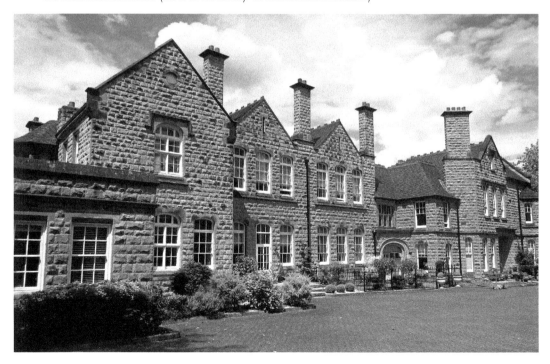

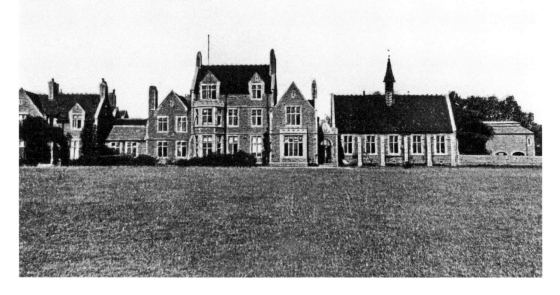

Boys' Grammar School, Mansfield

Queen Elizabeth's Academy

Established by royal charter in 1564, the original grammar school first opened in premises behind St Peter's, where it would remain, the nexus of coeducational schooling in Mansfield, until the school moved to a new site (*shown above*) in April 1878. Built by Giles & Gough of London with local stone, in the late nineteenth century, the school became 'boys only' as society demanded greater female emancipation. It would only be in 1993 that the facility reverted to being coeducational and, in an ongoing partnership with the Church of England, the school today enjoys academy status and is still housed in the same premises at the bottom of Linden Street. (*Above*: Courtesy of Mansfield Museum)

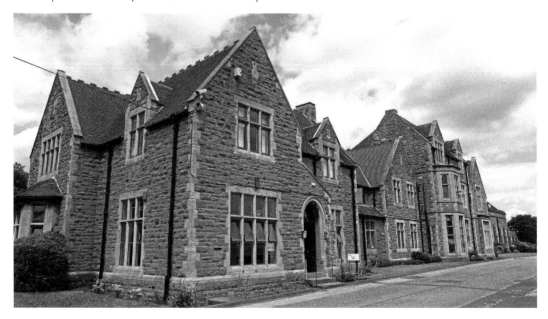

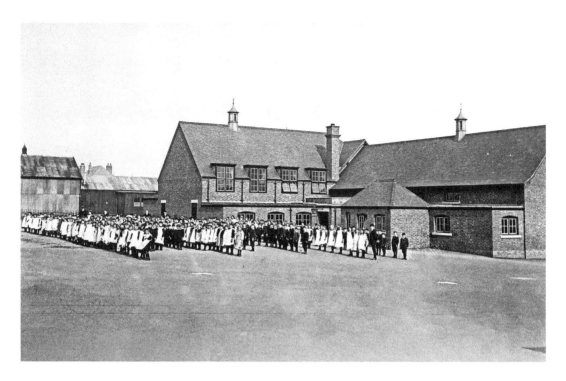

Forest Town Primary School

Uniformly attired boys and girls assemble in the 1906 school courtyard, shown above. Forest Town, on the north-eastern outskirts of Mansfield, owes its origin to the Mansfield Colliery, where coal was reached in 1904. Today, the paved road leading north towards Clipstone reveals little of the horrors of war that the impressionable young school pupils were exposed to a hundred years ago, when thousands of First World War troops marched through, and the bugled tones of the Last Post echoed down the school's corridors. (*Above*: Courtesy of Mansfield Museum)

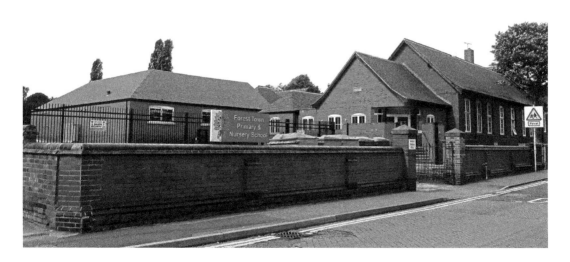

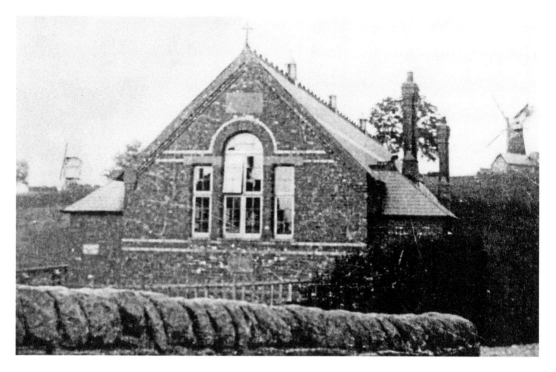

St Lawrence's School

A scratched, late-Victorian photo on the junction of Sandy Lane and Picks Hill speaks of a bygone age. The St Peter's mission building and the windmills on the ridge behind are now only historical memories. Demolished in 1992, and before St Lawrence Church was built on the opposite street corner in 1909, the building served as both a place of worship and a school. The new building on the same site (as *seen below*) still serves St Lawrence's pastoral mission in the form of a community centre. (*Above*: Courtesy of Mansfield Museum)

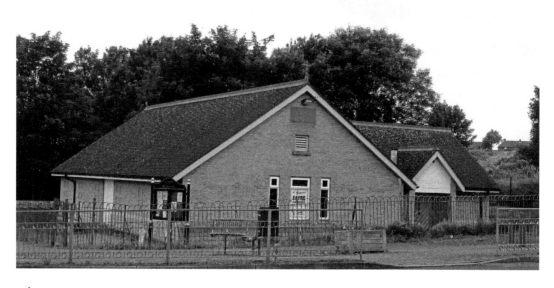

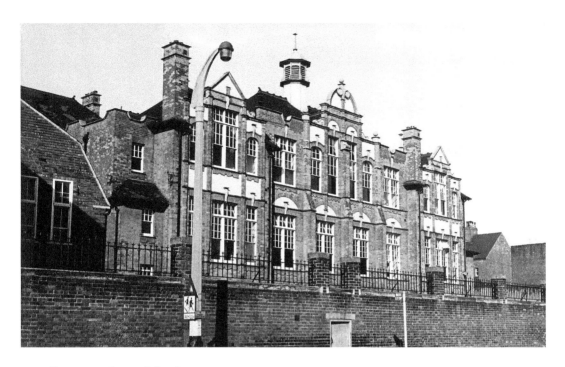

Rosemary Street Schools

In pursuance of recent government legislation opening elementary education to all children, and the subsequent raising of the school-leaving age, Mansfield's first school board was elected in November 1899. In December the following year, the board tabled the government inspector's report, which expressed concern that 'much care will be needed to secure uniformity of methods and work' following the establishment of separate boys, girls and infants schools from the 'old mixed' schools at the new Rosemary Street complex. In 2002, the buildings were demolished and private apartments were erected on the site. (*Above*: Courtesy of Mansfield Museum)

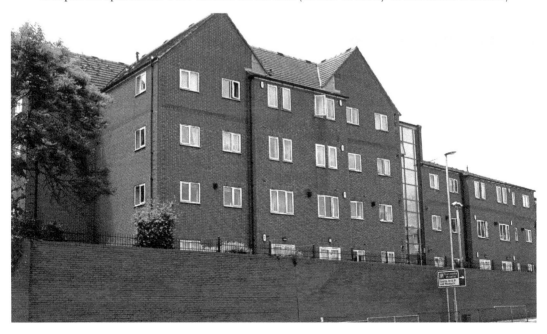

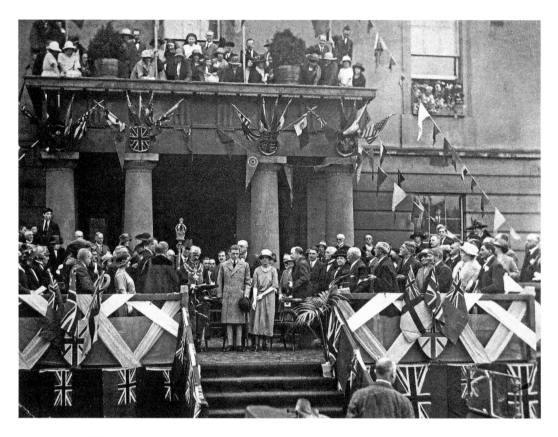

The Prince of Wales Visits

A demure Prince of Wales and future King Edward VIII is feted by Mansfield's citizenry as he stands at the town hall portals on 1 August 1923. Little was the prince to know that, thirteen years later, his love for American divorcee Wallis Simpson, and his resultant abdication, would precipitate constitutional upheaval and alter the Crown's lineage for all time. In 1999, following in the literal and figurative footsteps of his great-uncle, the current Prince of Wales (pictured *below*) pays the town a visit. (Both photos are courtesy of Mansfield Museum)

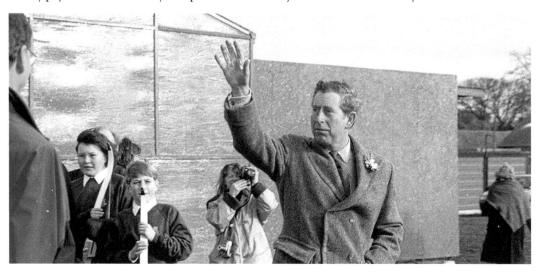

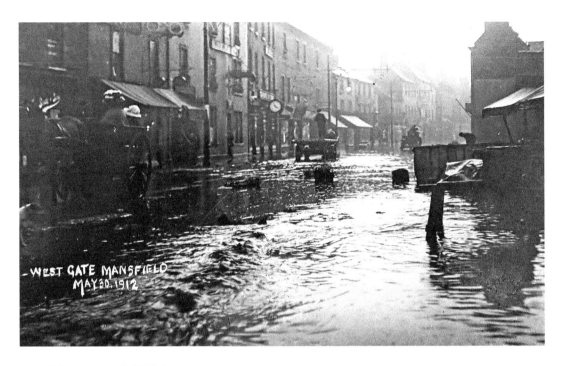

'River 40 Yards Wide'

The 31 May 1912 *Nottingham Evening Post* headlines the result of 1.46 inches of rain falling in the borough in the space of an hour: 'Shops were flooded, the pavement was torn up near the Eight Bells Inn, Church Street, garden produce, eggs, etc, floated down the stream in West Gate from the stalls occupied by the country women.' Now pedestrianised, the image of West Gate below still shows the rise down which the torrents had flowed more than a hundred years ago. (*Above*: Courtesy of Mansfield Museum)

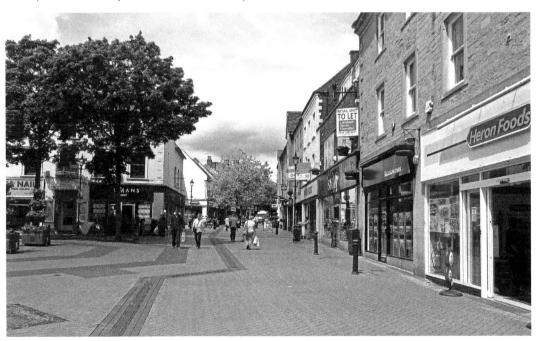

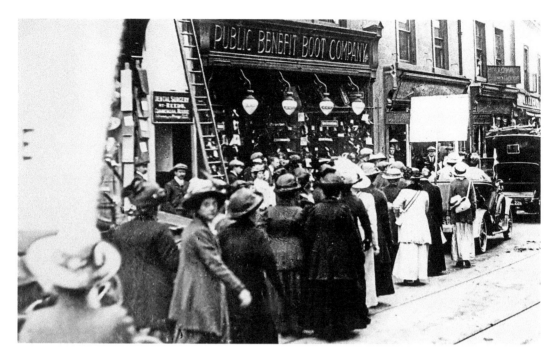

The Vote for Women

Determined placard-bearing members of the Mansfield Women's Suffrage Society demonstrate along Church Street, while seemingly bemused men on the pavement look on. In April 1906, the society's president, L. Wright, wrote to the parliamentary committee that had been debating a resolution, calling for sex to cease being 'a bar to citizenship', stating that she 'deeply deplores the action of certain occupants in the ladies gallery in causing unseemly interruption while the debate was in progress'. A new banking hall now stands at this point of the march. (*Above*: Courtesy of Mansfield Museum)

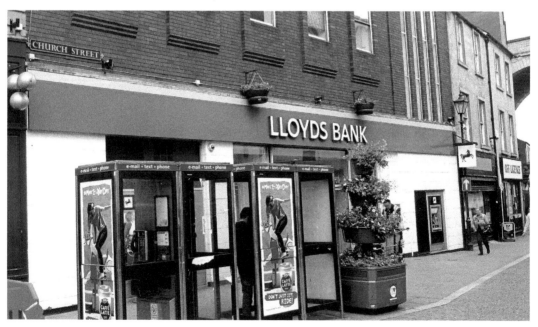

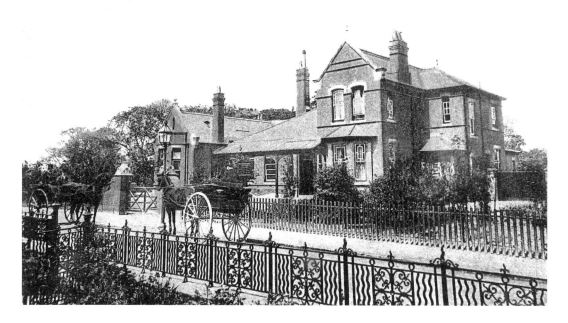

Accident Hospital

The colour-enhanced image is of the town's new accident hospital on West Hill Drive, which was opened on 27 October 1890 by the Duke of Portland. Built at a cost of £2,595, the facility started off with two wards and five beds. Accident victims would be admitted for free and would be cared for by a 'thoroughly trained and experienced nurse ... and a probationer under her'. Built in place of the Lawn Hospital, the photo below shows the same building well into the second half of the twentieth century, albeit sadly bedaubed with graffiti. (Both photos are courtesy of Mansfield Museum)

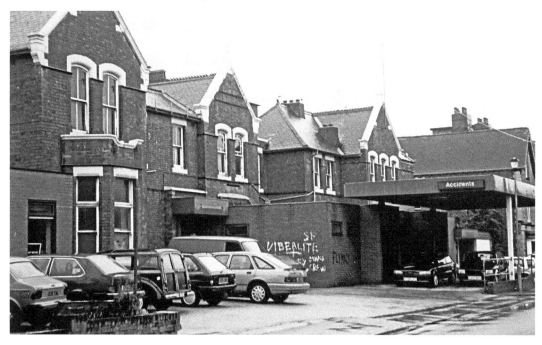

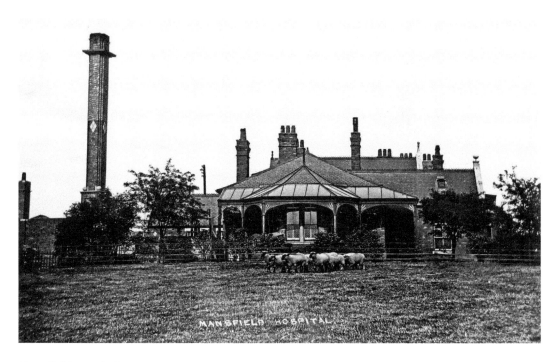

Mansfield Hospital

The tranquil pastoral setting no doubt assisted recuperation at the Mansfield Hospital. Today, the borough is served by the ultra-modern £320-million King's Mill Hospital, also sited with views over the rolling north Nottinghamshire countryside. The 550-bed facility treats 30,000 inpatients and 106,000 emergency cases annually. Opened in April 2008, one third of the hospital's heating and cooling requirements come from revolutionary surface-solar energy plates submerged in the adjacent King's Mill Reservoir. (*Above*: Courtesy of Mansfield Museum)

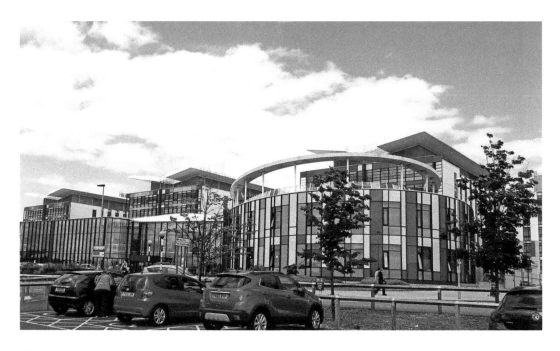

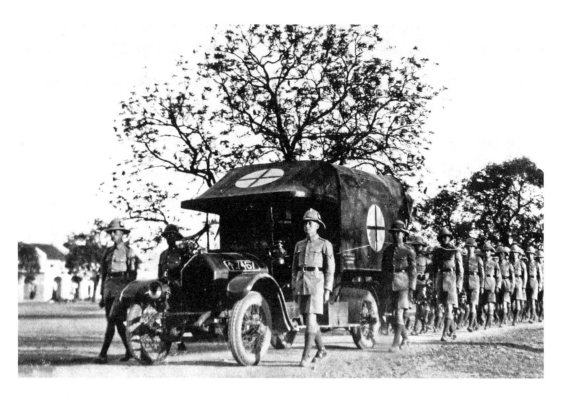

Ambulances Through Time

A First World War ambulance doubles as a hearse at this military funeral in Mansfield. At the time, such vehicles merely served to convey the injured as expediently as possible to the nearest medical care facility. In spite of this apparent basic mobile care, an appeal in August 1914 by the Mansfield Colliery Ambulance Division resulted in eighty-six miners volunteering for the Army medical corps. These modern, French-built ambulances at the King's Mill Emergency Centre carry the staff and equipment to immediately address trauma injuries on site, pending hospital admission – a far cry from those a century ago. (*Above*: Courtesy of Mansfield Museum)

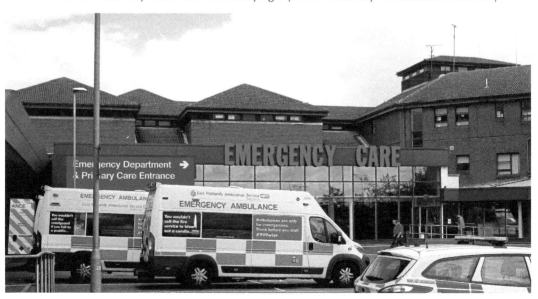

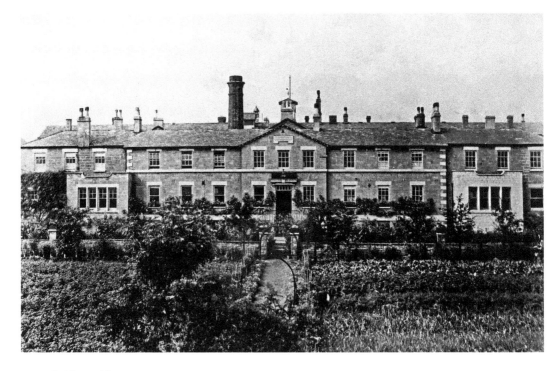

Mansfield Workhouse

In March 1915, at much the same time as the photo above, young workhouse resident George Woodward, described as 'an absolute schemer', was sentenced to twenty-one days with hard labour by the Mansfield magistrate for refusing to wheel stones. This was in spite of the fact that, while in police custody, he 'had tried to commit suicide by tying his braces and string around his neck'. This common mental disregard for thousands of paupers incarcerated in union workhouses throughout Britain came to an end in Mansfield at the final meeting of the Board of Guardians in March 1930. The building was demolished in 2007, and Mansfield Community Hospital – a rehabilitation facility – was erected on the site. (*Above*: Courtesy of Mansfield Museum)

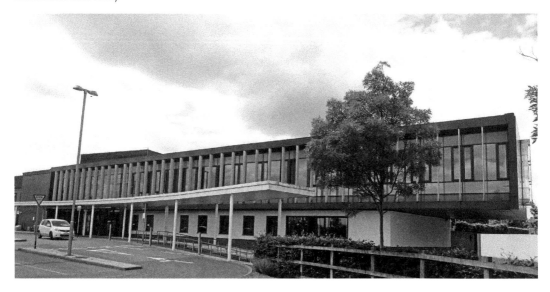

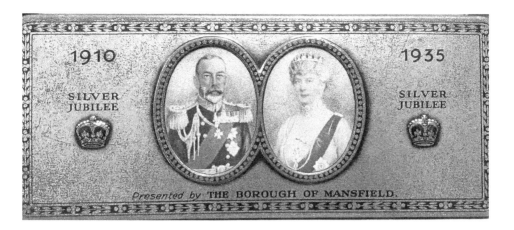

1910   1935

SILVER
JUBILEE

SILVER
JUBILEE

Presented by THE BOROUGH OF MANSFIELD.

Quality Tins

The manufacture of decorative tin boxes in Mansfield has its origins in the 1870s, when erstwhile tea salesman Robert Barringer started to pack mustard from his mill into tins handmade at the mill itself. Joined by his brother-in-law and son-in-law, the firm of Barringer, Wallis & Manners expanded rapidly as Players Tobacco and *Alice in Wonderland* author Lewis Carroll ordered from and endorsed the company. The commissioning of a lithographic printing machine in 1892 allowed for the manufacture of tins of a quality demanded by the Crown, especially for commemorative occasions. Gifts to British troops during the war in South Africa and the First World War were packaged in colourful Barringer tins. (Photos by the author, from the Mansfield Museum collection)

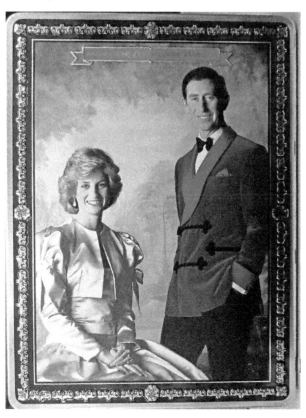

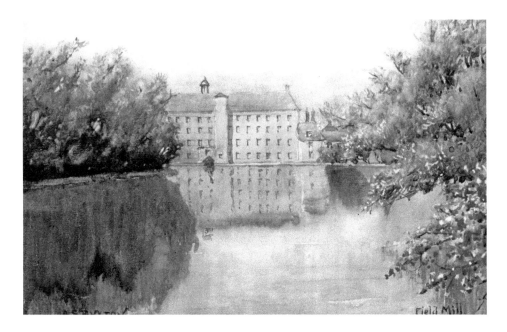

Field Mill

First built on the River Maun as a corn mill and driven by water from the river, in 1788 the mill was acquired by Nottingham Hosiery and converted to cotton spinning. The owners invested £1,000 in upgrading it and the capacity of the millpond was increased. The A. S. Buxton watercolour above portrays a rather romantic, but quite accurate, scene of the dam with the mill as a backdrop. Demolished in the 1920s, only a section of wall and the water intakes remain. The council has developed the pond into a nature reserve, a remarkable gem and haven for wild birds and waterfowl next to the football stadium. (*Above*: Courtesy of Mansfield Museum)

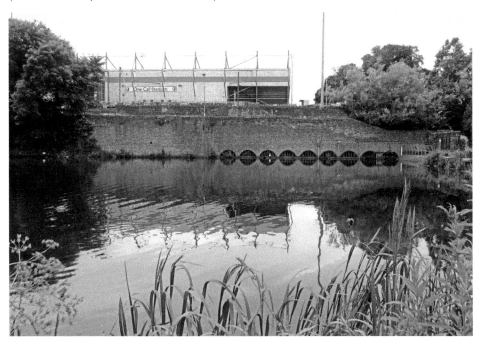

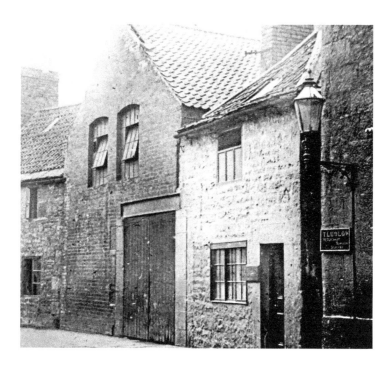

Leeming Street Foundry

Established in 1827 by a Samuel Midworth, Messrs C. and F. Sanderson took over the foundry premises, rented from the Duke of Portland, in the 1870s. Later known as Smith & Robinson, the company terminated its lease and moved to Hermitage Mill in 1903. The old foundry was demolished and, with 'one of the best streets in town', the Carnegie Library erected. The museum, now adjoining the library, was opened the following year. More than just an historical repository, the museum provides a wide range of community educational and outreach programmes in the building. (*Above*: Courtesy of Mansfield Museum)

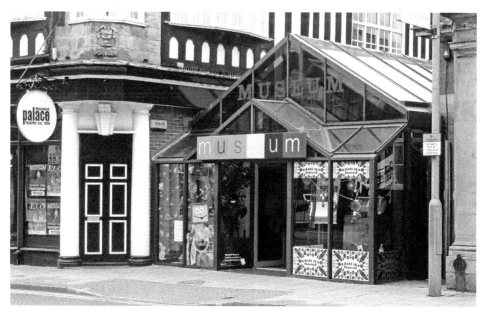

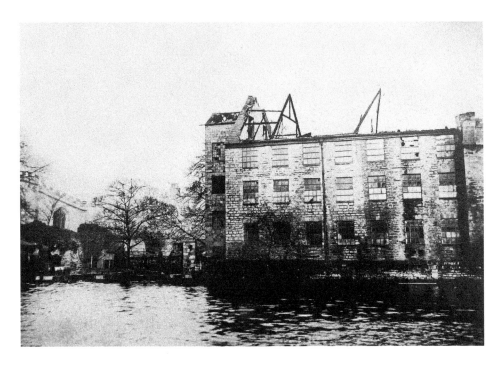

Town Mill

Built in the 1740s, the image above shows the devastation wrought by a 1907 fire to the top storey of the building. The second fire in a month in the mill owned by Messrs Bradley & Co., water was drawn from the River Maun and the dam behind the mill, and the fire doused in half an hour. A report carried in the *Nottingham Evening Post* the next day stated, 'The fact that the roof is match-boarded assisted the flames.' Subsequently restored and used as a warehouse and a live-music venue in the 1970s, a grant from the Heritage Lottery Fund was used to refurbish the mill, both inside and out, to conform to its original appearance. (*Above*: Courtesy of Mansfield Museum)

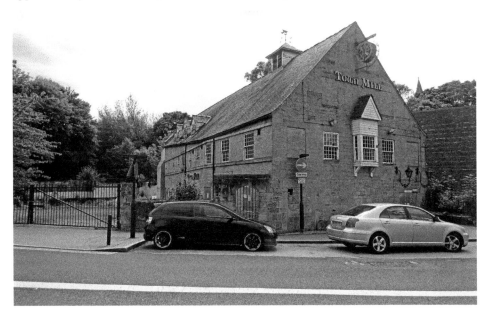

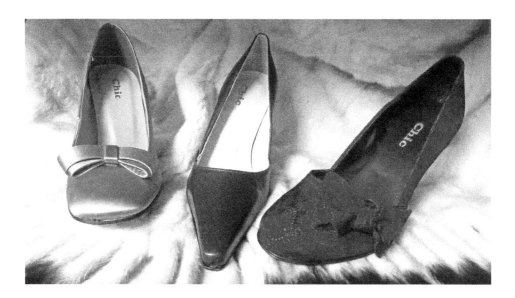

Boots and Shoes

In 1867, George Royce and John Gascoigne established a factory in Mansfield for the manufacture of boots. Some thirty years later, the partners split and Gascoigne, with help from his son William, formed the Mansfield Shoe Co. Bought out by management in 1981, the Mansfield Shoe Co. finally stopped production in 2004. The 'bewitching' Devonshire and more recent Chic (*above*) ranges of ladies' shoes are remembered by many. In 2007, the controversial 6-metre-high metal stiletto sculpture was unveiled on Quaker Way as a tribute to the town's shoemaking heritage. (*Above*: By the author, from the Mansfield Museum collection)

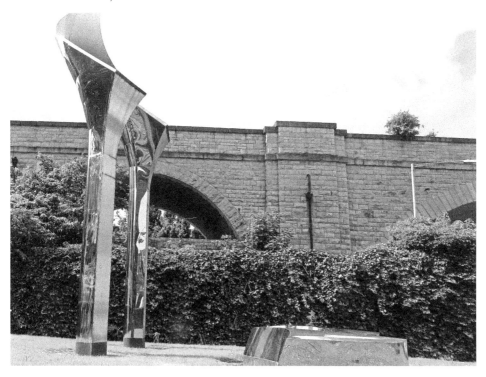

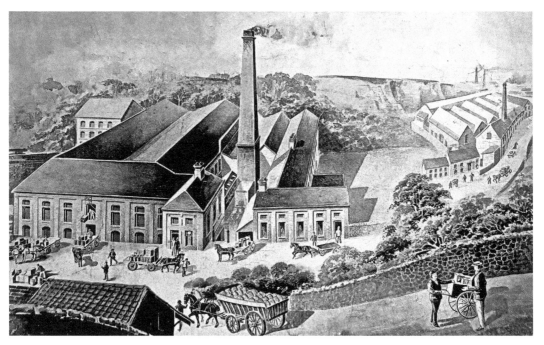

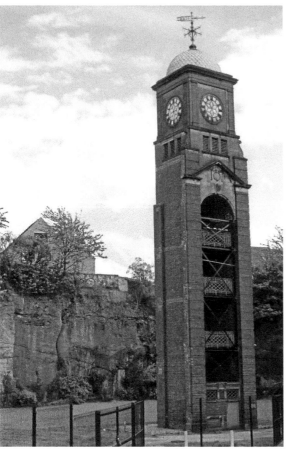

Rock Valley Works

The delightful drawing of the Rock Valley mustard mill, from 1862, depicts the factory where Barringer, Wallis & Manners went on to build a lucrative tin-manufacturing business. Colman's of Norwich subsequently acquired the mustard-milling business, and in 1918 the site was totally dedicated to making tin boxes for royalty, government and industry. In 1919, the tower block and clock tower foundation stone was laid. Today, this derelict landmark is all that remains of the once-thriving factory, the rest having been levelled early in 2010. (*Above*: By the author, from the Mansfield Museum collection)

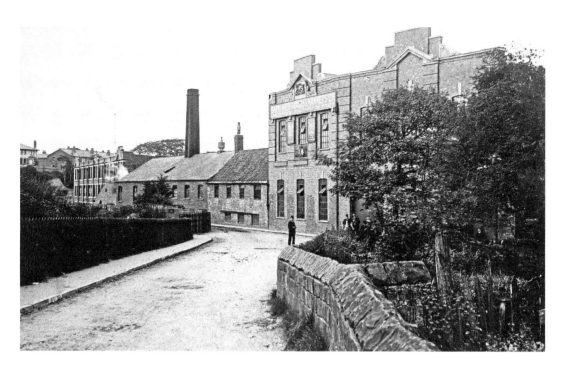

Metal Box

With its origins in Allied Tin Box Makers Ltd, by the Depression years of the 1930s, the tin can manufacturing Metal Box had become strong enough to survive the devastating global economic slump. Just before the Second World War, the company merged with Barringer, Wallis & Manners. The unparalleled wartime demand for its product allowed the company to add aerosol cans to its stable. Subsequent merges with French manufacturer Carnaud and Crown Cork & Seal saw Crown selling off the Rock Valley site and moving to new works on Crown Farm Way – Crown Speciality Packaging UK Ltd, shown below. The company still produces decorative tin packaging as one of its operations. (*Above*: Courtesy of Mansfield Museum)

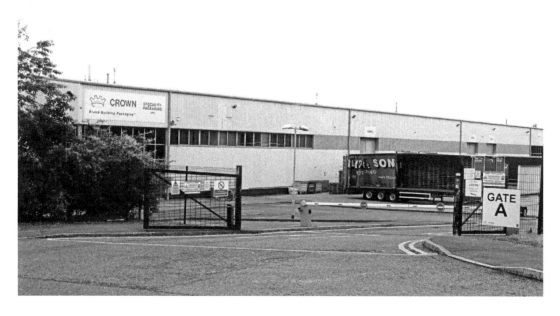

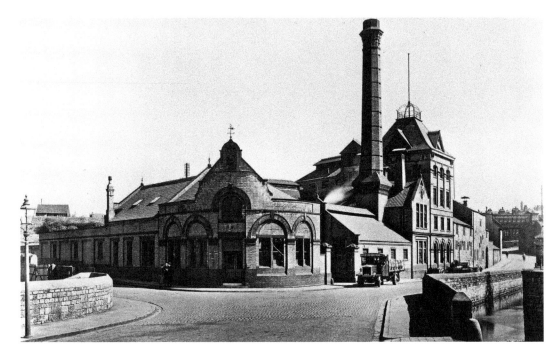

Mansfield Brewery

Situated at the bottom of Bath Street on Littleworth, Mansfield Brewery was formed when John Watson of Sheffield formed a partnership with farmer Samuel Hage of Ollerton and investor William Edward Baily, of Mansfield. By the turn of the century, the business was leasing seventy-two licensed premises – expansion which required the brewhouse to be rebuilt in 1907. With Mansfield Bitter developed as its signature brew, the brewery was bought out in 1999 and moved to Wolverhampton. The brewery itself was demolished in 2008, but the office block fronting Littleworth was spared. For a brief period, the Industrial Heritage Trust used the building for its Discovery Centre (*shown below*) until this too was closed in April 2015. (Courtesy of Nottinghamshire County Council www.picturethepast.org.uk)

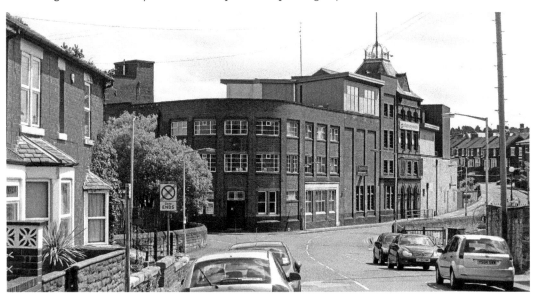

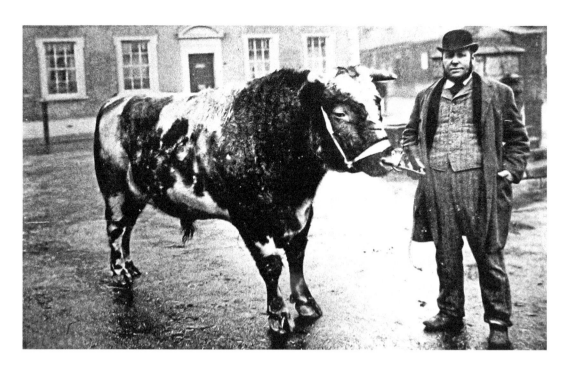

West Gate Cattle Market

Mr Collingham proudly shows off his prize bull, 'Prince', in the former cattle market on West Gate in August 1896. The cattle market moved to a new site on Nottingham Road in 1877. The steps and column of the Market Cross – also called the Buttercross – appear behind him. Dating from the sixteenth century, the sundial-topped cross (*seen below*) was restored in 2007, the surrounds paved and brightened with flowers. Standing next to the cross is the West Gate Water Pump, commemorating the first Methodist service in the town in 1788. (*Above*: Courtesy of Mansfield Museum)

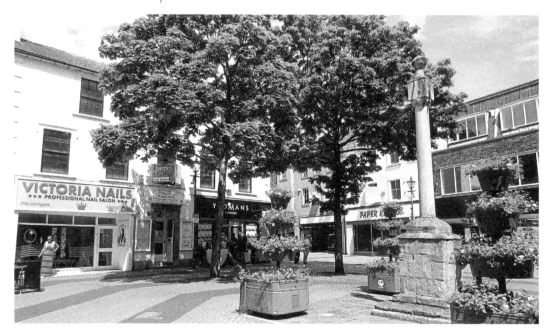

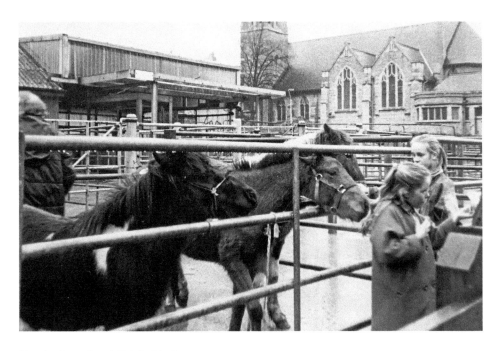

Nottingham Road Cattle Market

On a cold winter's day, *c.* 1980, ponies get treats at the cattle market on the corner of Nottingham Road and Bath Street. Having moved to this site from West Gate in the late 1870s, the market finally shut down in 1988 to make way for the Wet Leisure complex. In the background – clearer in the photo below – stands the 1913, Free-Gothic-style Methodist church. With its magnificent yellow-brick and ashlar façade, the unused building has just received planning permission to be converted into a restaurant. (*Above*: Courtesy of Mansfield Museum)

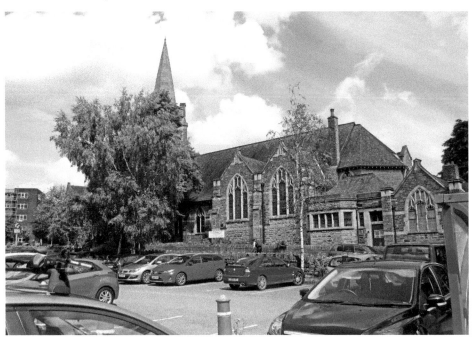

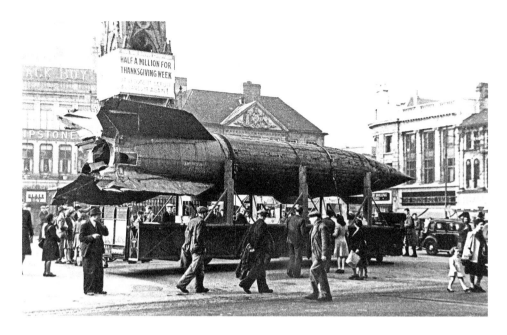

The Market Place

Reminiscent of a European market plaza, the Market Place has steadfastly, over hundreds of years, retained the status of the cultural and social centre of Mansfield. Market stalls, celebrations, and fairs and shows continue to characterise the square. In October 1945, a post-war 'Thanksgiving Week' campaign was launched to raise £500,000 towards the town's wartime contribution. The German 'vengeance weapon', a V2 long-range ballistic missile (*shown above*) forms a static display and centre of attraction. To this day, the Market Place has changed very little. (*Above*: Courtesy of Mansfield Museum)

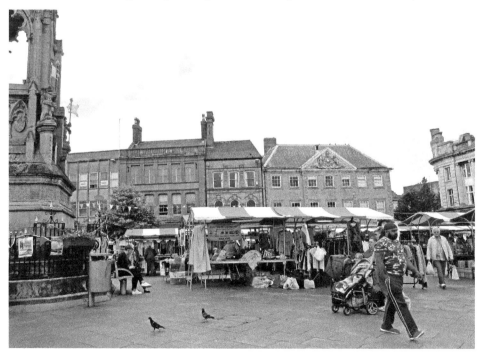

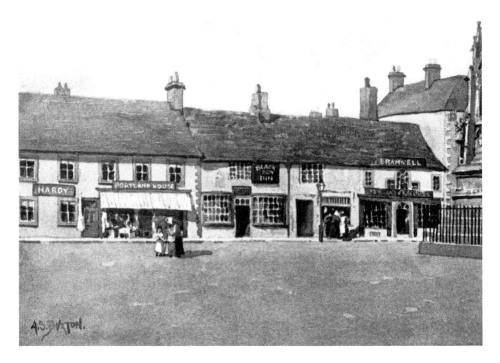

Small Business to National Chain

The brush of talented local artist A. S. Buxton captures the ambiance of turn-of-the-nineteenth-century Mansfield: buildings of thatch, stone, leaded windows, and local small businesses enclose the Market Place. While a few similar buildings still skirt the square, economic change forged by time gave rise to an unstoppable influx of national chains (*below*). However, in a town where small businesses still feature, it is ironic that some of these nationals have been unable to sustain profitable trading and have closed their doors. (Photo courtesy of Mansfield Library, www.picturethepast.org.uk)

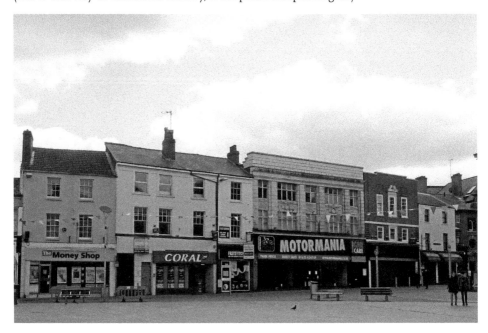

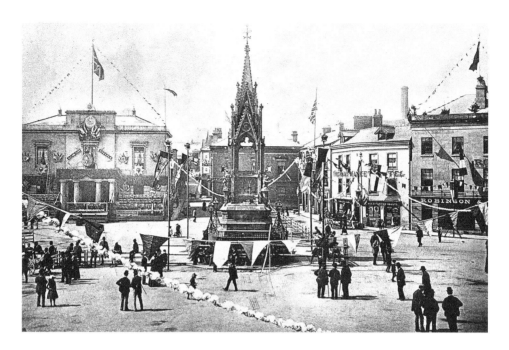

Bentinck Memorial

The erection in late 1849 of a memorial in the Market Place to Lord George Bentinck caused a furore among the self-styled Protectionists, who adulated the MP as the 'chivalrous champion of Protection' who stood up against the 'treachery of Sir Robert Peel' in scrapping the Corn Laws. His protagonists bemoaned the fact that his profound impact on social reform would go unrecognised on the Gothic Revival monument. Others contended that Bentinck's benevolence would have strongly favoured housing for the poor in his memory, and that 'he would spurn such a gewgaw, with all the contempt it deserves'. Restoration was carried out in 1979 and 1990. (Photo courtesy of Mansfield Library www.picturethepast.org.uk)

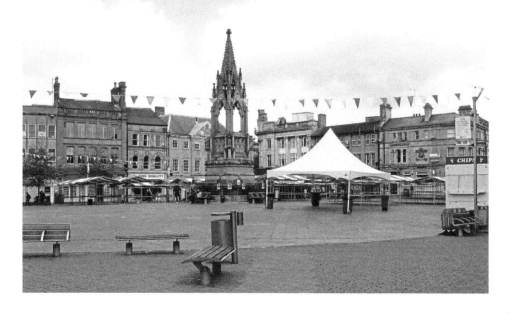

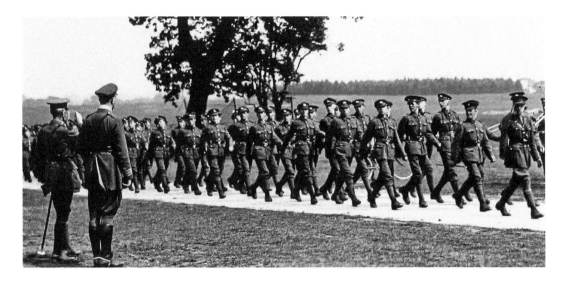

Into Combat

First World War soldiers march on parade at Thoresby Park, before being thrown into bloody barbaric battles on the Western Front. At the time, tented camps sprang up throughout northern Nottinghamshire, serving as divisional holding points prior to deployment. Seat of the Pierrepont family since 1600, battalions of the Sherwood Foresters also held their annual training camps at the site. Absorbed into the Mercian Regiment in 2008, the local descendants of those halcyon days at Thoresby are beckoned by the poster of a very different-looking twenty-first-century soldier to enlist as a reservist in the 4th Battalion at the Army Reserve Centre on Bath Street. (*Above*: Courtesy of Mansfield Museum)

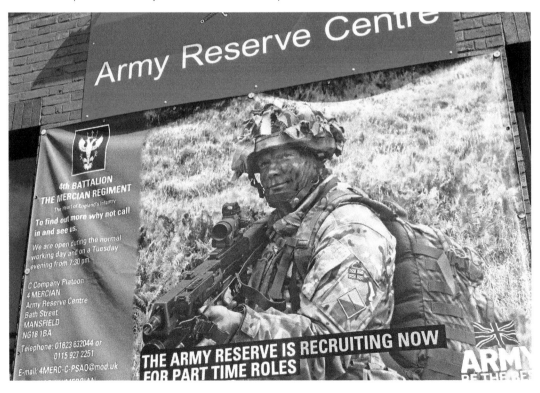

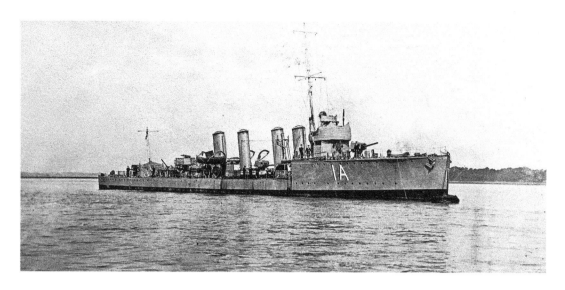

HMS Mansfield

In November 1940, Mayor H. Bageley received a letter from the destroyer's commanding officer requesting a plaque bearing Mansfield's coat of arms be made and placed 'in some conspicuous place, as a link with the town'. Today, that link with the Royal Navy is still thriving in the form of the Mansfield contingent of the Sea Cadets Corps. Working in partnership with the Royal Navy, the cadets meet twice a week at their Quarry Lane site. (*Above*: Courtesy of Mansfield Museum)

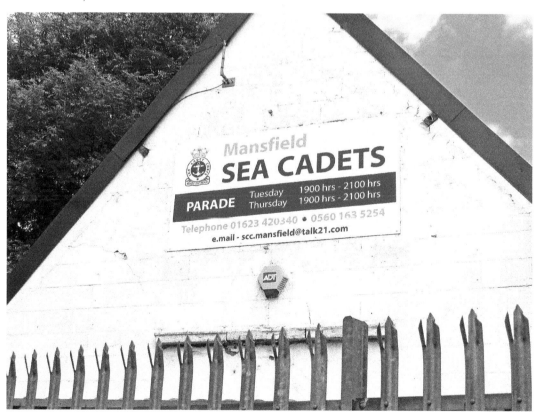

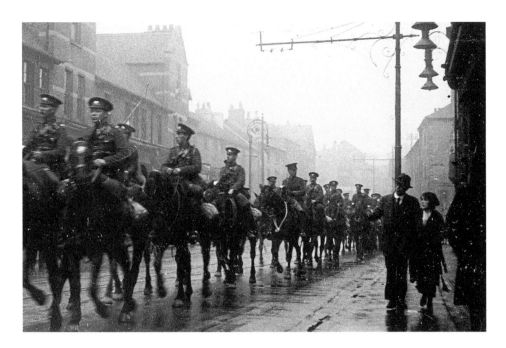

'Then let me ride my horses down in hell'

Mounted troops of the First World War ride along a rain-drenched Leeming Street. Many would never see their hometown ever again, lost or buried in the carnage of battlefields in France and Flanders. In 1917, the 6th Duke of Portland sold off Carr Bank Park so that Mansfield could provide its citizens with a lasting memorial to those who perished in the First World War. The curved-stone war memorial (*below*), with a bronze wreath, was unveiled on 4 August 1921: 'Their Name Liveth Forever More.' (Photo courtesy of Mansfield Museum and Art Gallery www.picturethepast.org.uk)

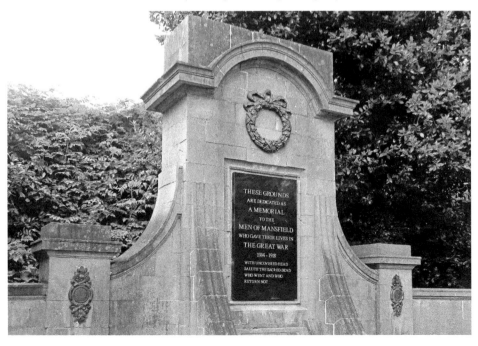

THESE GROUNDS
ARE DEDICATED AS
A MEMORIAL
TO THE
MEN OF MANSFIELD
WHO GAVE THEIR LIVES IN
THE GREAT WAR
1914 - 1918
WITH UNCOVERED HEAD
SALUTE THE SACRED DEAD
WHO WENT AND WHO
RETURN NOT

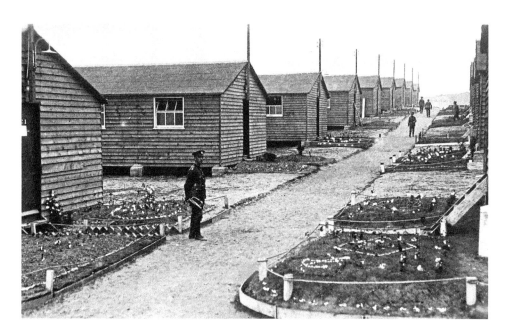

For Crown and Country

As the First World War developed into an uncompromising trench-based stalemate that cost the lives of tens of thousands, the War Office selected large swathes of forested countryside just to the north-east of Mansfield, in which to billet large numbers of Kitchener's New Armies. Most were tented billets, but a hutted cantonment was established and named Clipstone Camp, which accommodated 20–30,000 troops (*above*). Today, a modern brick building serves as a local recruiting office in Bath Street. Gone are the bell tents, wooden barracks and drill halls. (*Above*: Courtesy of Mansfield Museum)

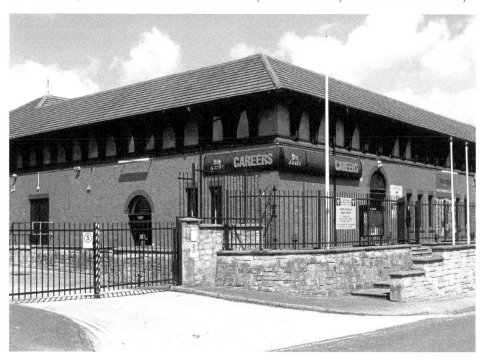

Best for War Pictures
The Weekly Guardian

Nottingham Evening Post

No. 11,454. (REGISTERED FOR TRANSMISSION IN THE UNITED KINGDOM)   TUESDAY, APRIL 20, 1915.   SIX PAGES.   ONE HALFPENNY.

V.C. FOR NOTTS MINER WHO CAPTURED 50 GERMANS

THE BATTLE ON THE HILL.

SIR JOHN FRENCH'S STORY OF THE BRITISH VICTORY.

LOSSES HEAVY ON BOTH SIDES.

SAILORS' GREAT GALLANTRY IN THE DARDANELLES.

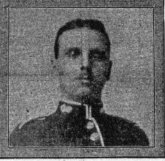

Lance-Corporal Wilfred Dolby Fuller, 1st Battalion Grenadier Guards, of Mansfield, awarded the V.C. for conspicuous bravery at Neuve-Chapelle.

MANSFIELD SOLDIER WINS THE VICTORIA CROSS.

CONSPICUOUS BRAVERY AT NEUVE CHAPELLE.

CAPTURED 50 GERMANS SINGLE-HANDED.

DUKE OF PORTLAND'S MESSAGE.

UNION JACK HOISTED AT MANSFIELD.

A Mansfield Victoria Cross

'No. 15624 Lance Corporal Wilfred Dolby FULLER, 1st Battalion Grenadier Guards. For most conspicuous bravery at Neuve Chapelle on March 12th [1915]. Seeing a party of the enemy endeavouring to escape along a communication trench he ran towards them, and, killing the leading man with a bomb, the remainder, nearly 50, finding no means of evading his bombs, surrendered to him. Lance Corporal Fuller was quite alone at the time.' Fuller, a Mansfield miner, passed away in 1947, but his memory and gallant actions are enshrined in this memorial in the Carr Bank Park.

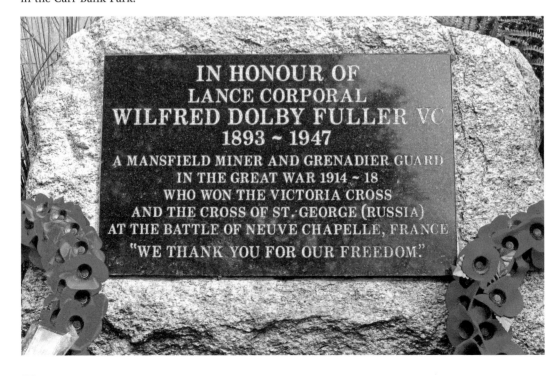

IN HONOUR OF
LANCE CORPORAL
WILFRED DOLBY FULLER VC
1893 ~ 1947
A MANSFIELD MINER AND GRENADIER GUARD
IN THE GREAT WAR 1914 ~ 18
WHO WON THE VICTORIA CROSS
AND THE CROSS OF ST. GEORGE (RUSSIA)
AT THE BATTLE OF NEUVE CHAPELLE, FRANCE
"WE THANK YOU FOR OUR FREEDOM."

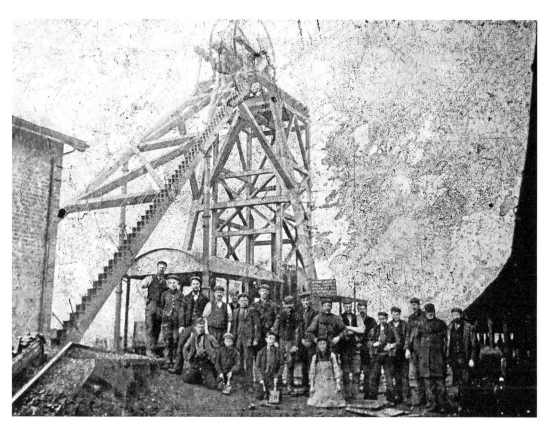

The Coal Miner

As Queen Victoria's long reign drew to a close, Nottinghamshire pits were being sunk, heralding the new era of coal mining. The coal miner was a special breed, enduring long, filthy hours in extremely difficult and dangerous conditions. The Pinxton Colliery miners (*shown here*) not only wore no protective gear, but young boys were among their number. This bronze statue on St Peter's Way stands as a tribute to the 35,000 British mineworkers who 'kept Britain moving for more than 100 years'. Created by Nikolaos Kotziamanis, the sculpture was unveiled on 20 October 2003. (*Above*: Courtesy of Mansfield Museum)

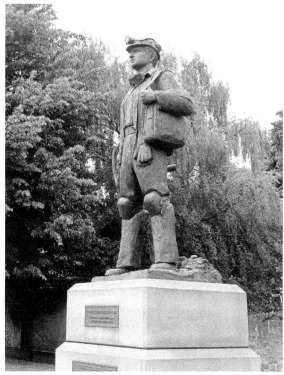

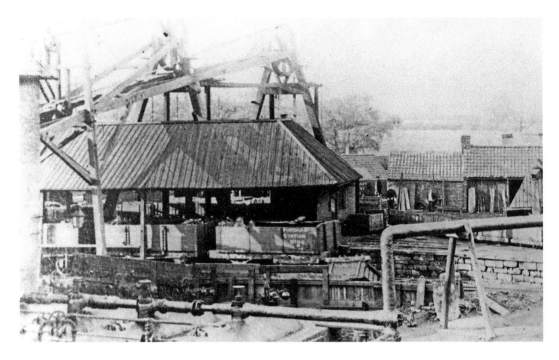

Pitheads

Wooden early twentieth-century pitheads at Pinxton Colliery's Nos 1 and 6 shafts hide the numerous dangers the miners faced underground. On 14 January 1909, eighteen-year-old William died a painful death when his jacket was caught in the cogwheels of a compressed-air engine, dragging him between the revolving cogs. In April 2003, the Clipstone Colliery (*shown below*) finally closed after a period of limited production. The Clipstone Colliery Regeneration Group Ltd has submitted a proposal to convert the headstocks, as they are known locally, into a thrill-seekers attraction. (*Above*: Courtesy of Mansfield Museum)

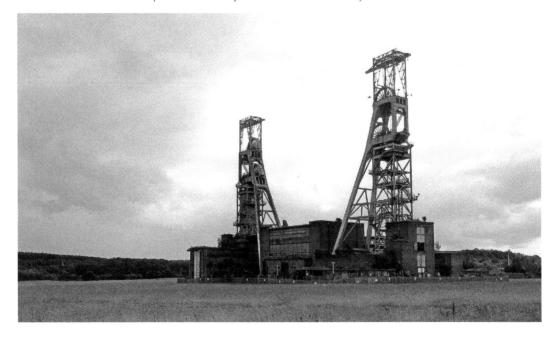

SAFETY HELMETS FOR MINERS

Their Value Demonstrated

At an inquest at Forest Town to-day on George Davidson, 32, of 9, Eighth-avenue, Forest Town, who was suffocated under two tons of coal at Mansfield Colliery on Tuesday, the coroner (Lieut.-Colonel H. Bradwell) showed the jury a safety helmet which the man was wearing at the time.

The helmet, which was still on deceased's head when he was extricated, was undamaged, except for a small dent in the brim, and had prevented any head injury.

" This shows how very useful these helmets are," he said, " and it should impress that fact on miners generally. I understand that this colliery company insists upon helmets being worn, but at some pits I believe they are not compulsory."

Miner's Safety

This report of the proceedings of a coroner's inquest into the accidental death of Mansfield Colliery miner George Davidson appeared in the *Nottingham Evening Post* on 26 May 1939. The coroner himself, Lieutenant-Colonel Bradwell, showed the jury the unfortunate man's helmet which he was wearing at the time when 2 tons of coal engulfed him. Bradwell pointed out that had Davidson not suffocated, he would have survived as his helmet had prevented him from sustaining any cranial injury. Miner safety equipment, crude and long neglected, had become an effective statutory requirement. (*Below*: Photo by the author, from the Mansfield Museum collection)

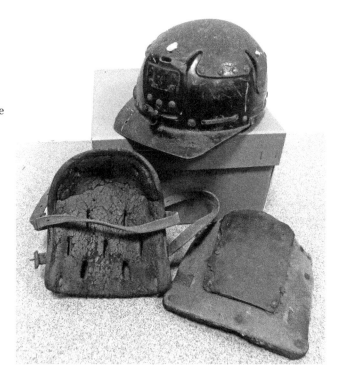

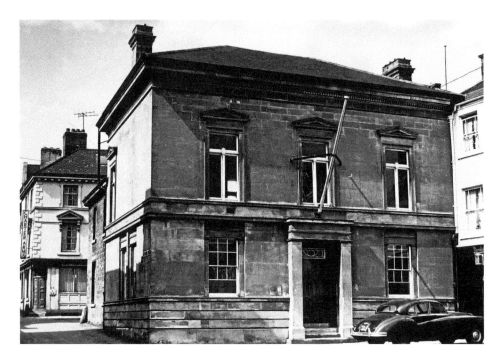

The Court House
Built in the Market Place in 1840 as a savings' bank, the building became the county court in the 1860s. The premises ceased to be used as a court when the new Magistrates' and County Court building was opened on Rosemary Street in 1996. The image above was taken in 1964, when cases were still being heard, usually before a county judge from Nottingham. In May 2016, Wetherspoons made the decision to sell the concern. The sandstone building has since become a free house. (*Above*: Courtesy of Mansfield Museum)

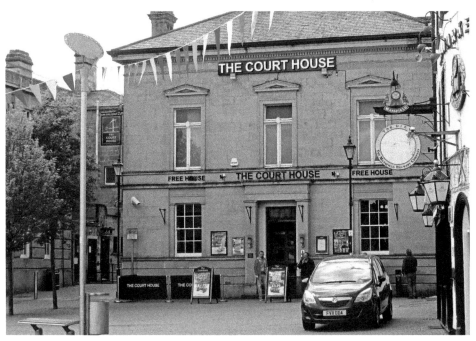

The Old Eight Bells

The original seventeenth-century building, and former residence of local philanthropist Samuel Brunts, was later occupied by a carpenter and church warden by the name of Robert Watson, who opened its doors as a beerhouse in 1832. Watson was responsible for the construction of some of the windmills that once lined the top of Skerry Hill. To assist St Peter's and St Paul's to complete the church's peal, Watson donated a bell. It is believed that this was the origin of the name of his house and later the public house. The Eight Bells (*shown below*) is in fact one that was rebuilt on the site in 1925. (*Above*: Courtesy of Mansfield Museum)

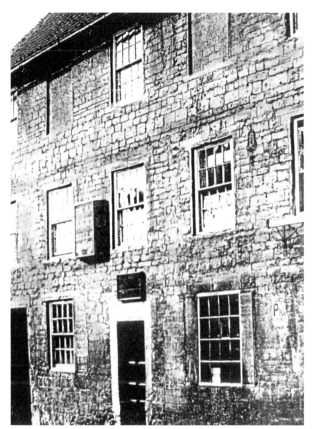

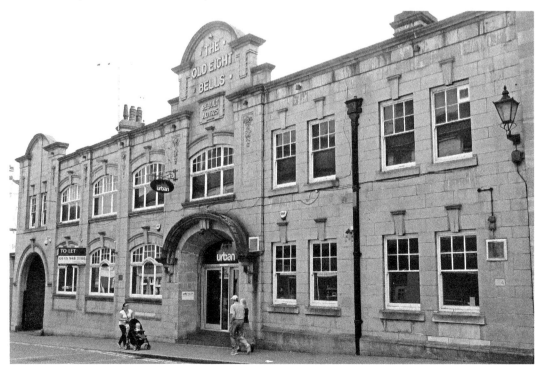

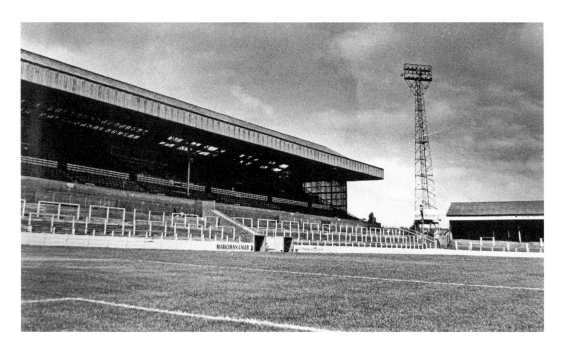

The Field Mill Stadium

Deriving its name from the adjoining mill, the Field Mill football ground has the reputation of being the oldest football field in the world to host professional games. First used in 1861, the Mansfield Greenhalghs beat Eckington Works in an 1892 FA Cup tie. For a short period in the 1980s, the Mansfield Marksman rugby league team shared the stadium. In 1999, the west stand was demolished and the two-tier stand (*pictured below*) was erected. Resplendent in the Stags' amber and blue livery, the 10,000-seat One Call Stadium, as it is known today, stands proud of surrounding homes at its site on Quarry Lane. (*Above*: Courtesy of Mansfield Museum)

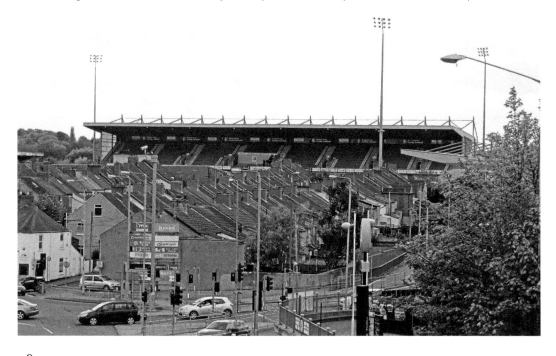

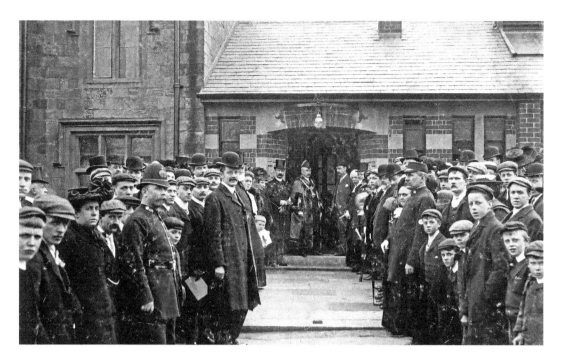

Public Swimming Baths

Mayor John Edward Alcock prepares to open the new 'handsome' public baths on Bath Street on a chilly afternoon on 16 April 1904. Reported as another addition to the list of public buildings made by the 'progressive Corporation of Mansfield', the project cost £6,800. Demolished relatively recently in 1990, the Water Meadows Swimming and Fitness Complex (*below*) was opened across the road, on the site of the old cattle market, to provide a state-of-the-art facility. The town's love for water had an enormous boost when local girl Rebecca Adlington won three gold medals at the 2008 Olympic Games in Beijing. The swimming centre on Westdale Road was proudly named after her. (*Above*: Courtesy of Mansfield Museum)

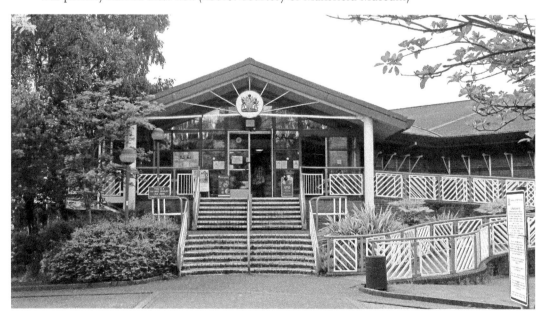

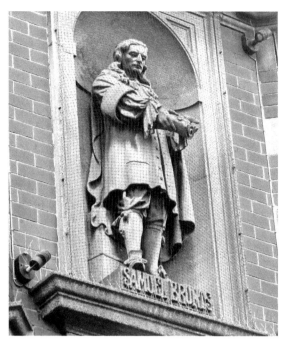

Sculptures

In a town where artistic talent is cultivated and allowed to flourish, seventeenth-century philanthropist Samuel Brunts appears to gaze down on the fruits of his munificence. The statue stands in a round-headed niche on a 1915 building at the corner of Toothill Lane and Leeming Street. In sharp contrast is the highly polished stainless-steel, 13-metre-tall feather sculpture, known as *A Spire for Mansfield*. Positioned in 2007, this Wolfgang and Heron public art is intended to remind the town of its coal-mining heritage and the canaries once taken underground to detect lethal gases.

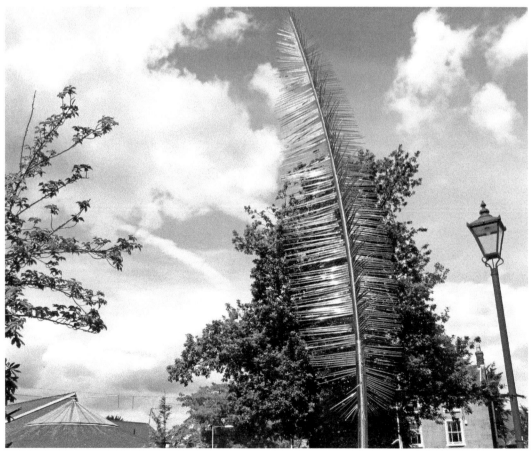

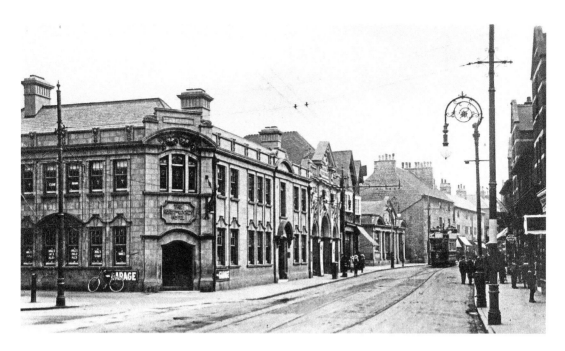

The Horse and Jockey

Records indicate that the first Horse & Jockey existed on Leeming Street in 1778. In 1903, this section of the thoroughfare was sold for redevelopment and the landlord, Abraham Heston, closed down his inn. In 1909, a public house was rebuilt on the site. Apart from some unsightly twenty-first-century embellishments, the stone façade and arched doorways remain unchained. The current tenants operate a bar and restaurant, featuring traditional and Mediterranean cuisine, in an interior tastefully 'remodelled, restyled and reborn'. (*Above*: Courtesy of Mansfield Museum)

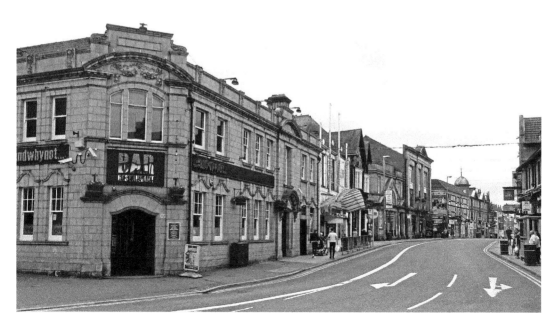

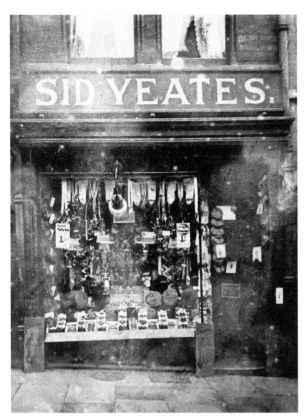

The Small Trader

Arguably, one of the most enduring characteristics of Mansfield is the prevalence of individually owned and run shops, operating still from the same small premises of a bygone age. Sid Yeates was one such 1908 shopkeeper, his packed shopfront window attesting to his profession as 'tailor, hosier and gents outfitters'. His son Jack took over running the store until the 1980s, when he disposed of the business. In 2010, Mr Harris purchased the premises and Sid Yeates closed its door for the last time. On the same street, a nail salon shows that today the small trader still has a place. (*Above*: Courtesy of Mansfield Museum)

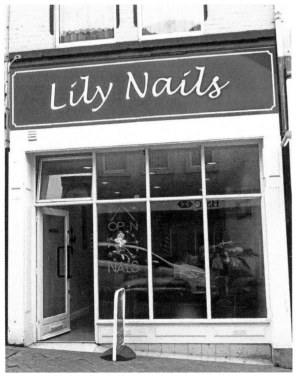

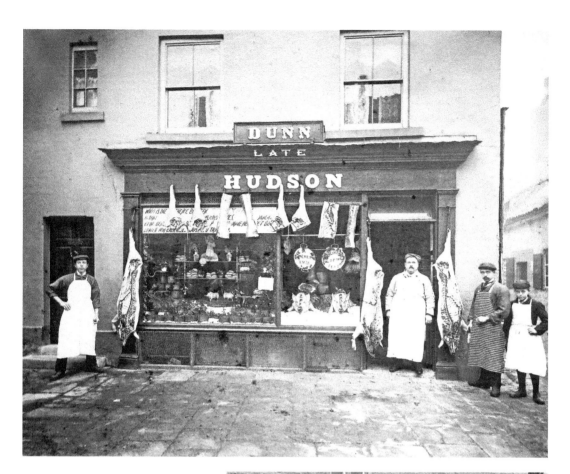

The Family Butcher

Decades may separate these two butcheries, but only the dictates of modern health regulations have shaped the front of the contemporary blue and cream shop on Bridge Street: outdoor merchandising. In February 1906, secretary of the Mansfield and District Butchers' Association, Mr J. T. M. Dunn – most likely a connection with the name on the shop above – gave evidence at the borough police court at which a butcher was found guilty of selling pig's 'pluck' (offal) that was badly contaminated with tuberculosis. The man was fined £1 and costs. (*Above*: Courtesy of Mansfield Museum)

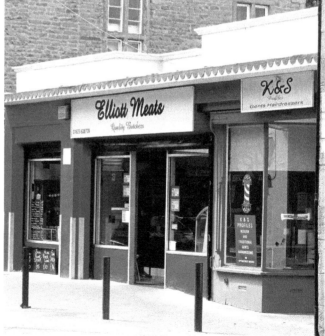

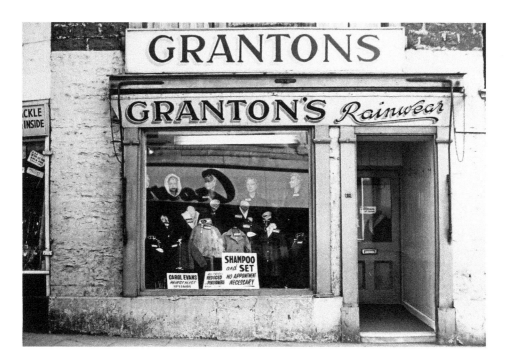

No. 62 West Gate

It is not unusual to find small, individually listed premises in this market town, such as No. 62 West Gate, a status granted in 1955. It is officially described as two houses: late seventeenth century and mid-eighteenth century with late twentieth-century alterations – the building was restored in 1989. The 1962 photo of Granton's epitomises the diversity of trade offered by shopkeepers then and now, and is suggestive of prevailing personal attention. The owners of a butcher and delicatessen are now the custodians of this old stone building. (*Above*: Courtesy of Mansfield Museum)

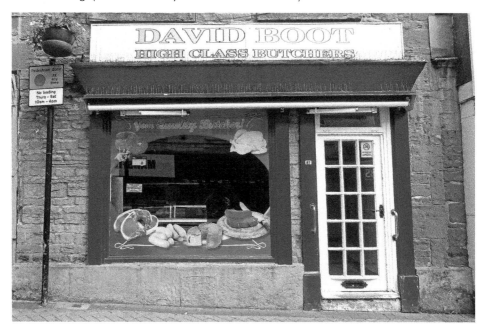

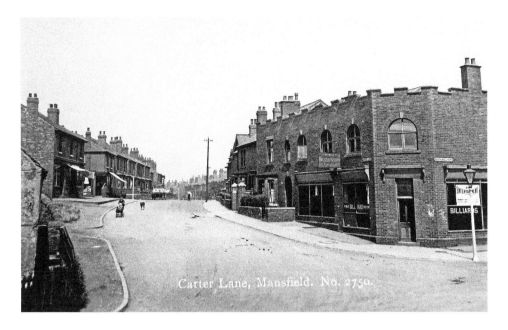

Carter Lane Billiard Room

On 8 March 1911, builder Martin Morris applied for a licence to operate a public billiard room in an upstairs room of a building on the corner of Carter Lane and Southwell Road. The applicant was granted a licence, but failed in his bid to 'close the room not later than 1 a.m'. Deputy Mayor J. H. Collins, at the bench, was reported to have retorted, 'I should think not, indeed.' The licence, under further advice from Supt Rogers, stipulated the room had to close at 11 p.m. That building is now barely recognisable: the erstwhile billiard room windows are boarded up, the brickwork painted, and the crenellations bricked in. (*Above*: Courtesy of Mansfield Museum)

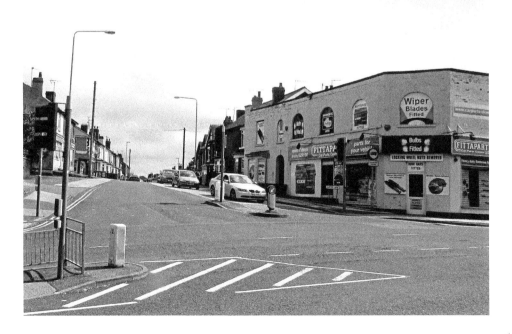

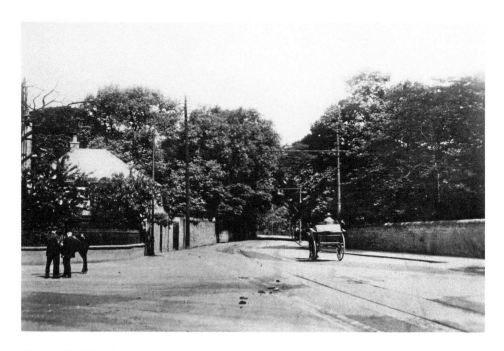

Chesterfield Road

Horses – and their calling cards – and horse traps characterise a relaxed-looking Edwardian Chesterfield Road. The 1906 photo, shows the tramline which had only been installed the previous year. The 9 June 1905 *Nottingham Evening Post* reported that 'the first tramcars have arrived at Mansfield, and at about three o'clock this morning the engineer made a trial trip on the completed section in the Chesterfield Road'. The road has undergone dramatic transformation since then; it is now a dual carriageway cluttered with street furniture and traffic lights. (*Above*: Courtesy of Mansfield Museum)

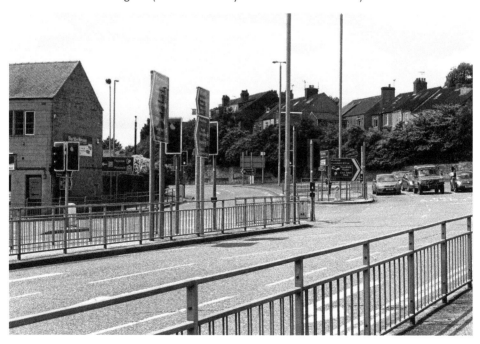

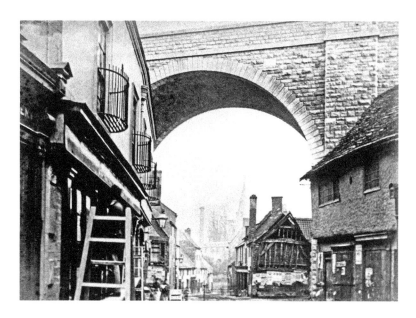

Church Street

Church Street is straddled by an arch in the Mansfield to Worksop Railway viaduct in this 1871 photo. The industrial smokestack and St Peter and St Paul's spire appear as a ghost-like backdrop. When compared to the 2016 image (*below*), it is very evident that few of the buildings have survived the vagaries of time and prosperity. Most notable is the decrepit wooden-framed structure on the corner with White Hart Lane. Conveyance records show that a William Edmund Pegg sold the property to James Henry Blake in August 1893. Between 1911 and 1925, jeweller and optician John Christopher Craven Brittain was the proprietor. (*Above*: Courtesy of Nottinghamshire County Council www.picturethepast.org.uk)

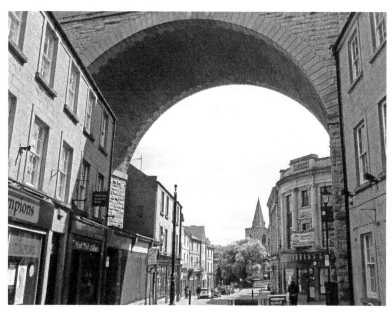

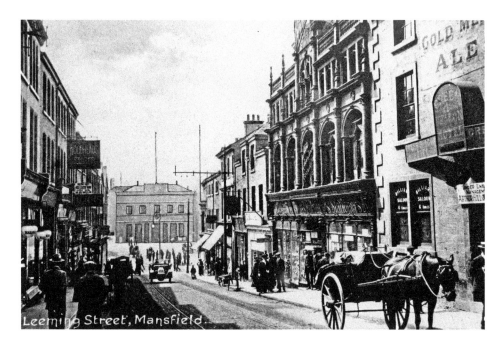

Leeming Street

An early 1900s street scene, with tramlines tracking down Leeming Street to the Market Place. The photographer's attempt at manually defining the outlines of the town hall is conspicuously inaccurate. The flanking buildings have changed little: the now-vacant Boots building is still presenting architectural beauty (*below*) amid a relatively dull assembly of angular stone and brick edifices. With horses, chugging motor cars, and trams a distant town memory, Leeming Street is now paved and largely pedestrianised. (*Above*: Courtesy of Mansfield Museum)

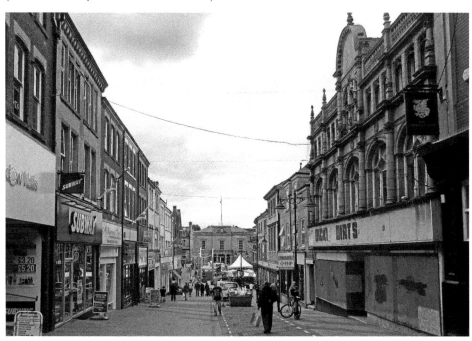

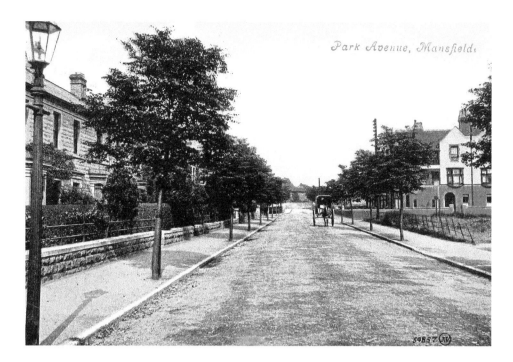

Park Avenue

A lonely horse and trap, making its way along a wide, tree-lined Park Avenue in around 1907, epitomises the pedestrian pace of suburban Mansfield of this time. Having just passed Park Court on their left, the driver makes his placid way towards the junction with Woodhouse Road. A white twenty-first-century automobile now also approaches Park Court with the same red-brick and plastered walls residence on the corner. Would it be fanciful to imagine that these same trees have survived more than 100 years? (*Above*: Courtesy of Mansfield Museum)

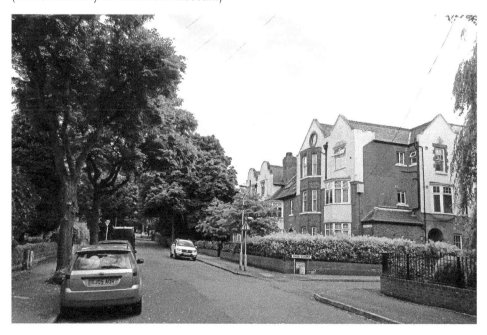

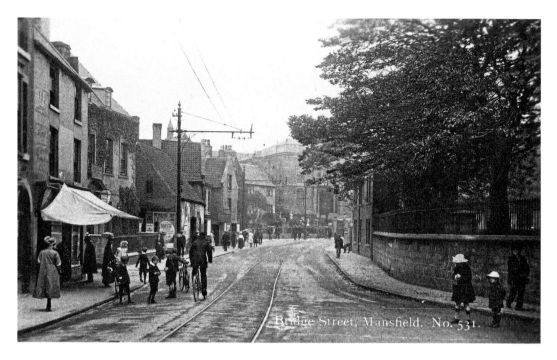

Bridge Street

Sunday-best attired boys and girls amuse themselves on an early 1900s, tramlined Bridge Street where it meets Church Side. The railing-topped stone wall skirts St Peter's and St Paul's, while the imposing Bridge Street Methodist Church looms in the middle distance. Apart from the building having been demolished where Elliott Meats now trades, the same buildings still stand along this stretch of Bridge Street, including the one of stone adjacent to the Methodist Church, a white-painted sundial prominent on its façade. (*Above*: Courtesy of Nottinghamshire County Council www.picturethepast.org.uk)

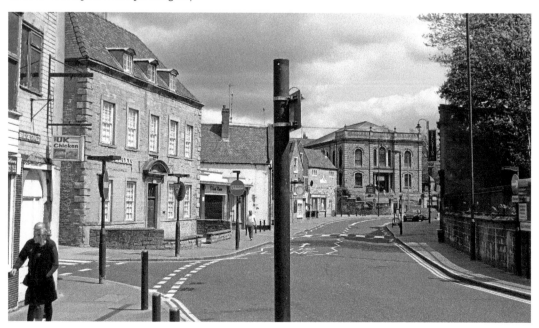

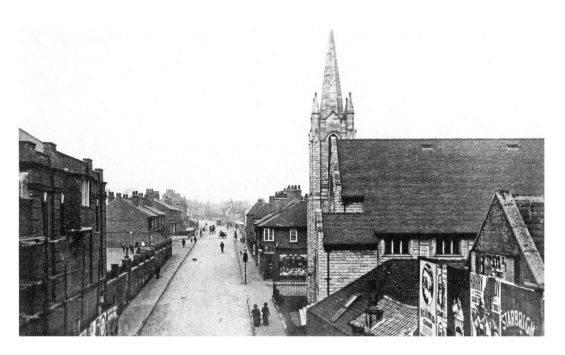

Rosemary Street

A narrow Rosemary Street in 1916 boasts the four-year-old Methodist Church, with its landmark Gothic steeple. A poster in the right foreground promotes Icilma Cream for ladies, which, among other properties, was 'made specially to prevent the growth of superfluous hair'. Rosemary Street has since become a dual carriageway. In July 1974, the Methodist Church was levelled and the congregation moved to a new building near the Civic Centre at the top of Rosemary Street. (*Above*: Courtesy of Mansfield Museum)

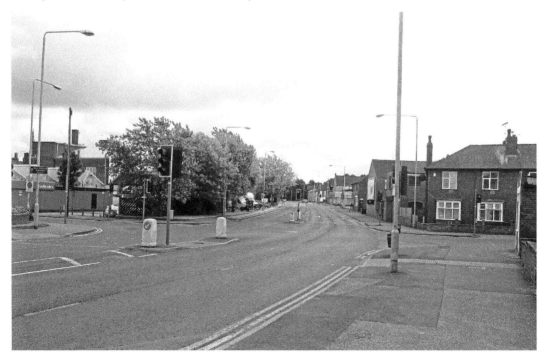

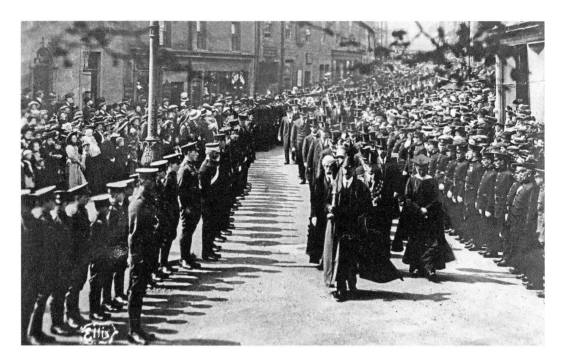

Albert Street

'Members of the Corporation, the yeomanry, territorials, fire brigade, cadet corps, lads' brigades, boy scouts, and others line a crowded Albert Street in November 1909 as the mayoral procession wends its way towards the Market Place and town hall. Leading the parade is the mace-bearer, shouldering the borough mace. In November 1902, the council agreed to use the surplus of the Mansfield Coronation Fund (Edward VII), an amount of £94 11s, to purchase a mace 'suitably engraved as a permanent memorial of the Coronation'. Messrs T. and J. Bragg of Birmingham were commissioned to manufacture the mace. (*Above*: Courtesy of Mansfield Museum)

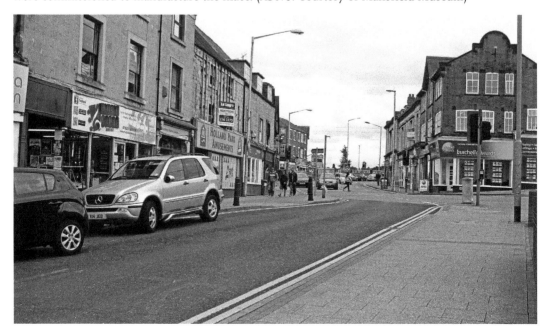

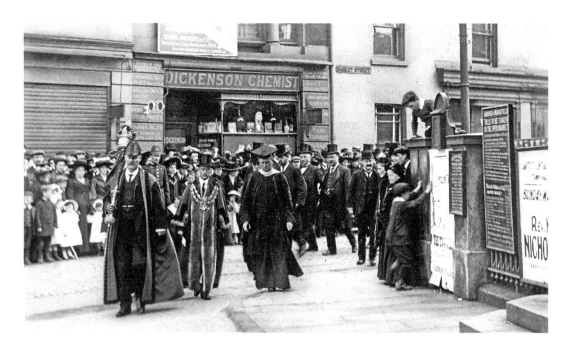

Mayor's Sunday

Sunday 21 November 1909, and a week later than planned (owing to the death of Alderman J. H. Blake) Mayor J. H. Collins trails the mace-bearer at the head of 'an exceptionally long' procession, described as 'quite an imposing affair'. Returning from a service at St Peter's Church, where the national anthem was sung, the service was conducted by Revd C. H. N. Ivens, with the sermon preached by Canon Prior. The Dickenson Chemist building, behind the procession as it approaches the steps of the town hall, has since been replaced by a Georgian-style brick building from where a jeweller and pawnbroker now operates. (*Above*: Courtesy of Mansfield Museum)

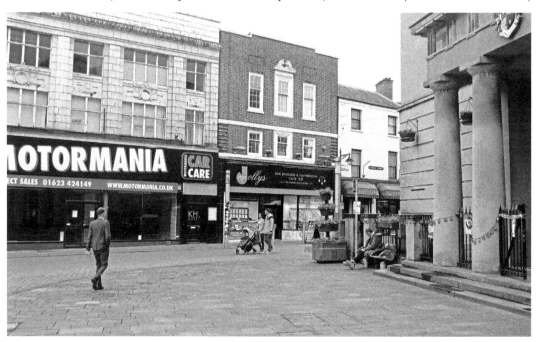

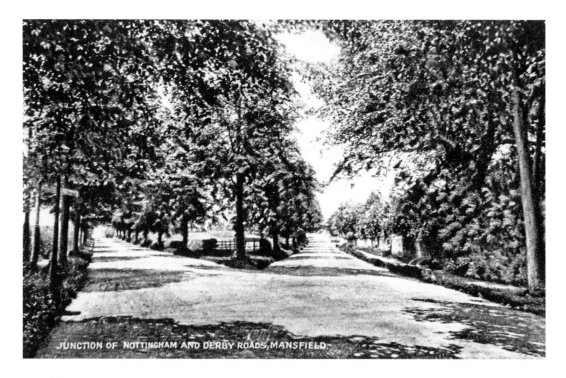

An Old Junction

Over a century ago, the meeting of the arterial roads from Derby and Nottingham angled together in what can only be described as a rural setting. Realigned, and trees cleared, the junction of these two roads is now the site of the £24 million redeveloped Vision West Nottinghamshire College. Founded in the 1970s, the college offers post-16 diplomas and degree courses to some 30,000 full- and part-time students from the whole spectrum of industrial sectors. Dubbed 'a living piece of social infrastructure', grey-, sand- and red-coloured Proteus panels clad the stunning, award-winning, abstract and geometric campus buildings. (*Above*: Courtesy of Mansfield Museum)

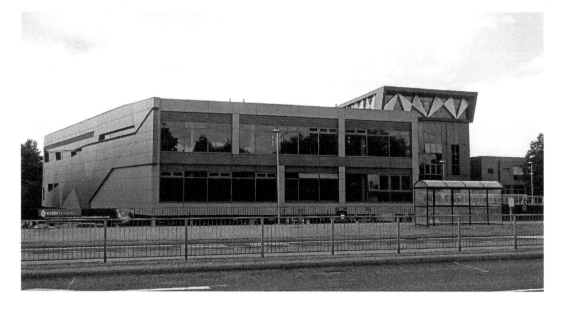

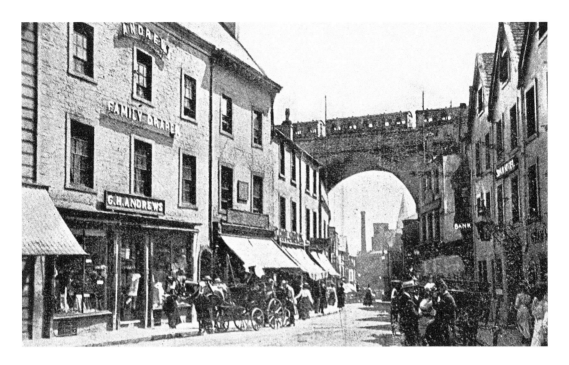

A Train Passes Over

A passenger train plies the route out of Mansfield atop the railway viaduct, seen here over Church Street in the early 1900s. The Andrews Family Draper experienced some drama one evening in August 1916, when a soldier on leave, William Miles, hurled his boots through the shop's plate-glass window. After arresting Miles, who confessed to the deed, PC Richards was told, 'I was a long way from sober.' The building no longer exists, a modern brick building now in its place, which provides a banking hall for Lloyds. (*Above*: Courtesy of Mansfield Museum)

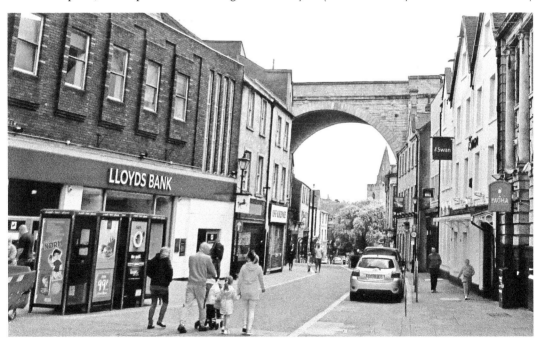

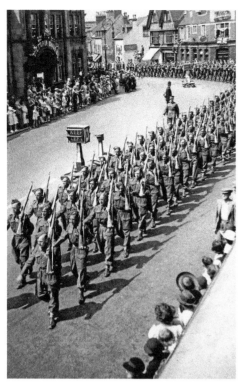

'Back Your Boys'

Guest of honour, First Lord of the Admiralty A. V. Alexander took the salute on 21 June 1941 as a column of soldiers, shouldering 303 rifles, led a long procession of 'military and civil defence organisations, savings groups, and many other organisations ... with tableaux and bands'. The occasion was the start of Mansfield's 'Back Your Boys' week-long campaign to raise £200,000 in war savings. The troops are seen marching past the Victoria Hotel on Albert Street. Today, the same sash-windowed, stone building is used as a steakhouse, grill and bar, retaining the monarch's name. (*Left*: Courtesy of Mansfield Museum)

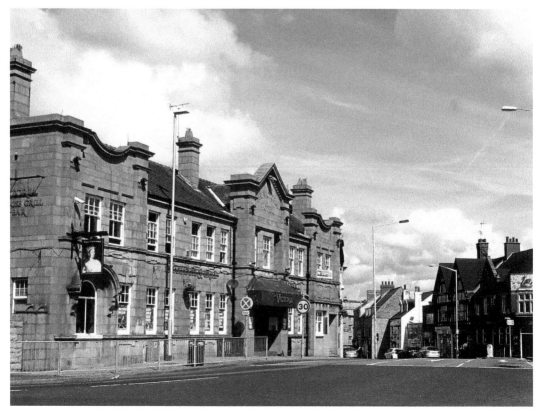

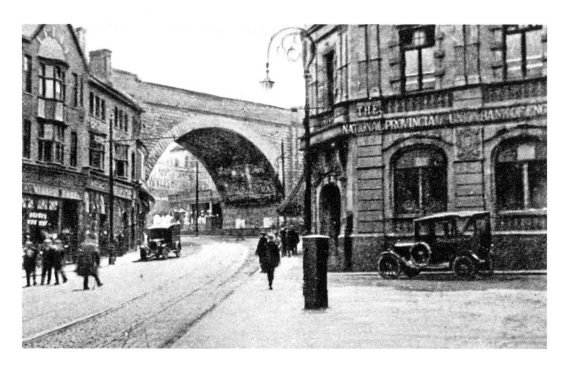

Market Street

The eye is drawn along tramlines that curve up Market Street and through the ubiquitous railway viaduct. To the right is the clumsily titled National Provincial & Union Bank of England, shortened in 1924 to the National Provincial Bank. Operating from 1833, it merged with the Westminster Bank in 1970, resulting in 3,600 NatWest branches throughout the country. Formerly the Metz Bar, the Byron public house now occupies this ashlar and brick, Renaissance Revival listed building. (*Above*: Courtesy of Mansfield Museum)

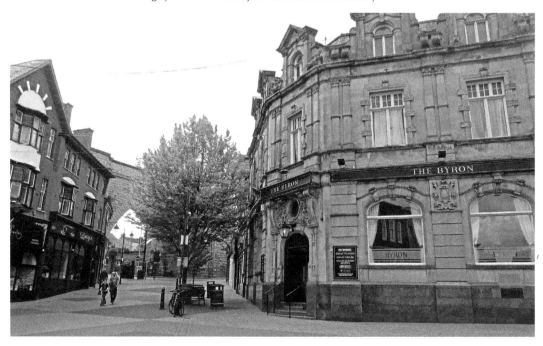

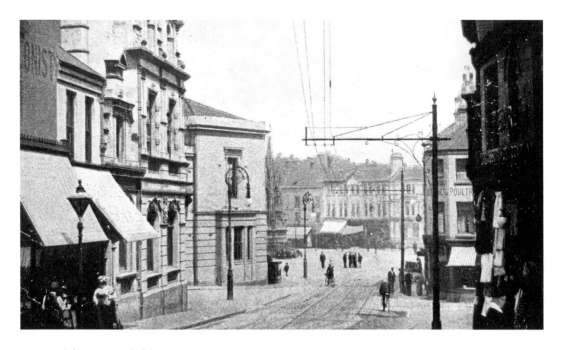

Postcard from Mansfield

The 1920s colour keepsake reveals a view down Market Street towards the Market Place – the Bentinck Memorial is visible peeking out behind the town hall. Directly behind the pole carrying the tram pantograph contact wires, the corner building houses a butcher shop, one of many in the town that placed a strong emphasis on livestock marketing. At the 1929 Christmas Fat Stock Show, the town's first female mayor, Mrs E. E. Wainwright, performed the traditional auction of the champion beast 'in quite the brisk professional style'. A shop offering beauty treatment and services for men and women now operates at this site. (*Above*: Courtesy of Mansfield Museum)

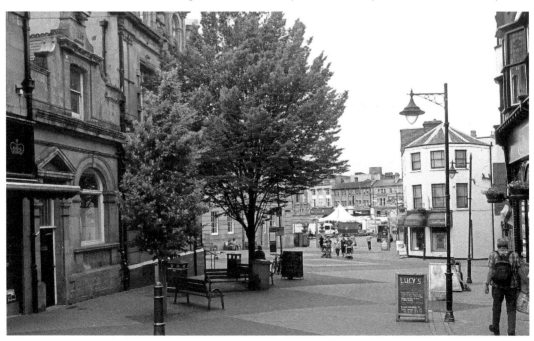

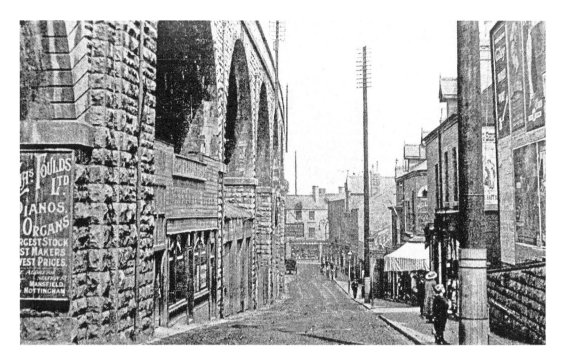

White Hart Street

A young lad studies posters on a wall in this 1917 cameo of White Hart Street. Established in Nottingham in 1893, the musical instrument family business, Charles Foulds, also had branches in Mansfield, Lincoln, Heanor and Derby, with the latter still thriving more than 120 years on. The 1875 Midland Railway's viaduct, with grand arches and rock-faced ashlar facing, towers over the narrow lane as it slopes down to Church Street. The viaduct underwent restoration work in the late 1900s. (*Above*: Courtesy of Mansfield Museum)

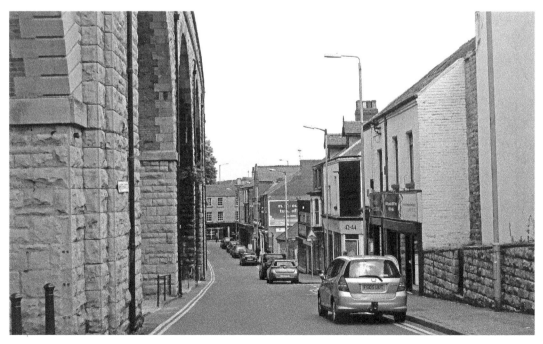

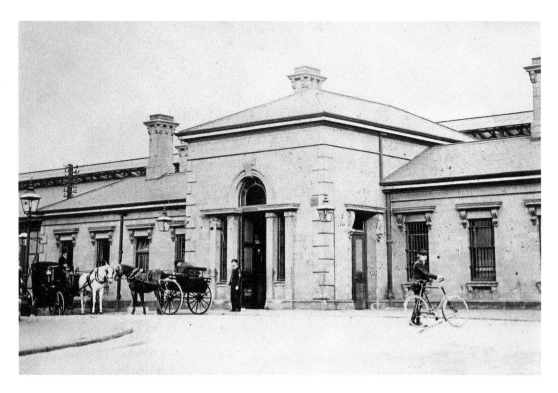

Midland Railway Station

Not to be confused with the former Great Central Railway's Central Station, this rail terminus was acquired by the Midland Railway to extend the line from Leen to Mansfield. Tenders for the construction of the station went out in June 1849. It was long regarded as a branch line; however, in October 1964, the station was closed and acquired by Brunel's and converted into a bar. The reconnection of the Nottingham–Worksop Robin Hood line in 1995 resuscitated the terminus, resulting in the station being bought back, faithfully refurbished and reopened in 2001, timeless in appearance. (*Above*: Courtesy of Mansfield Museum)

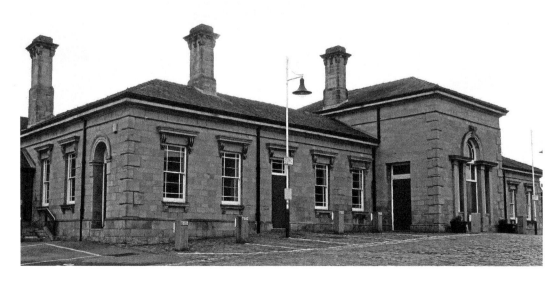

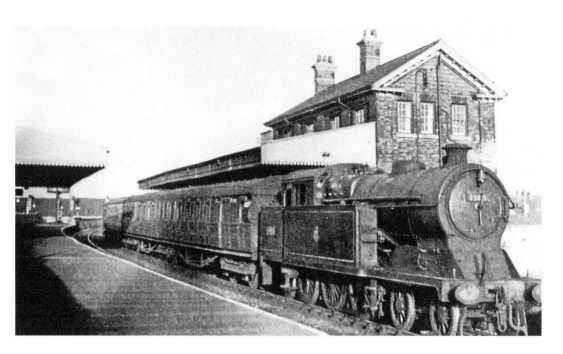

Rail Travel

A BR class 9N 4-6-2T Great Central Railway (GCR) locomotive chugs out of Mansfield's Central Station sometime in the early 1900s. The GCR built twenty-one of these John Robinson-designed locomotives at the Gorton Works, near Manchester, between 1911 and 1917. A hundred years later, an East Midlands Trains Class 156 Super Sprinter rolls to a stop at the refurbished Midlands Railway Station in Mansfield. The diesel multiple-unit train (DMU) is one of 114 built by Metro-Cammell between 1987 and 1989 at the Washwood Heath works in Birmingham. (*Above*: Courtesy of Mansfield Museum)

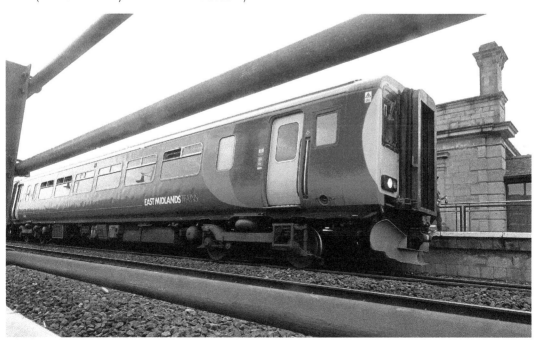

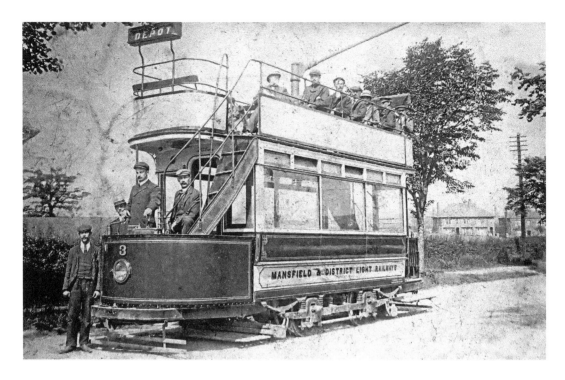

Urban Commute

The Mansfield & District Light Railways operated electric trams in Mansfield from 1905 to 1932. Using cream and red liveried cars, the network consisted of five routes covering around 12 miles. Number 3, shown here, was built by Hurst Nelson and Co. Ltd of Motherwell, becoming one of the town's first twelve open-top tramcars. A super-low-floor, wheelchair-friendly, Alexander Dennis Enviro 200 bus (one of sixty operated by Stagecoach in Mansfield) moves off from a stop on Bridge Street. (*Above*: Courtesy of Mansfield Museum)

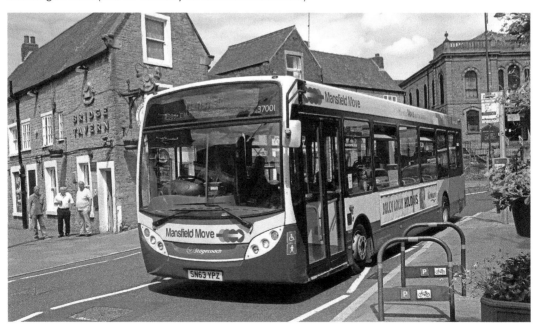

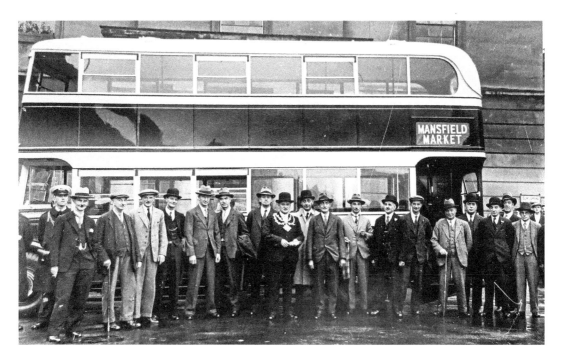

Double-Deckers

In September 1932, the 'long anticipated exchange over from trams to motor buses' saw the Mansfield Traction Co. invest in forty-five double-deckers, each with a capacity of fifty-six passengers. Mayor J. Pollard inspected the first sixteen of these buses, drawn up in a line across the Market Place, saying 'Mansfield will possess one of the finest fleets of up-to-date double-deckers owned by any provincial operator.' The double-deckers remain popular. The original AEC Regent services are now offered by ALX 400s, such as this one at a stop on Leeming Street. (*Above*: Courtesy of Mansfield Museum)

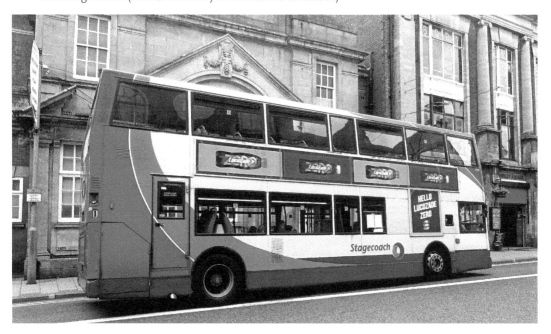

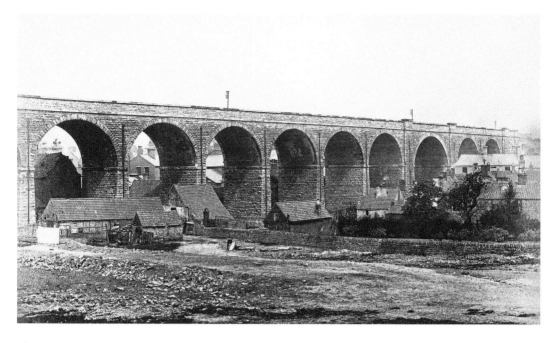

The Railway Viaduct

Bisecting the town centre, the fifteen-arch railway viaduct was completed in 1875 as the final stage of the Midland Railway's line to Worksop. Given Grade II-listed status in April 1975, the brick arches are faced with stone ashlar. In the photo, the rundown croft and line of buildings along the viaduct delineate the course of the future White Hart Street. In its history, the viaduct arches have, at various times, provided enclaves for the siting of small-scale traders, such as the pottery decoration studio seen below on White Hart Street. (*Above*: Courtesy of Nottinghamshire County Council, www.picturethepast.org.uk)

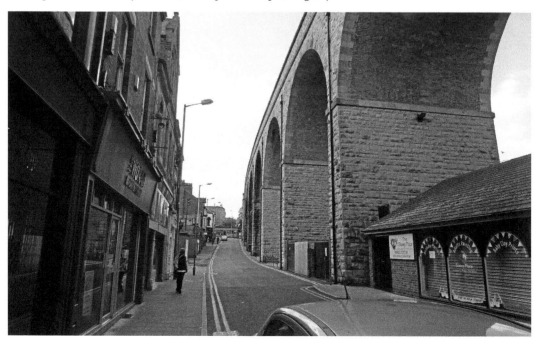

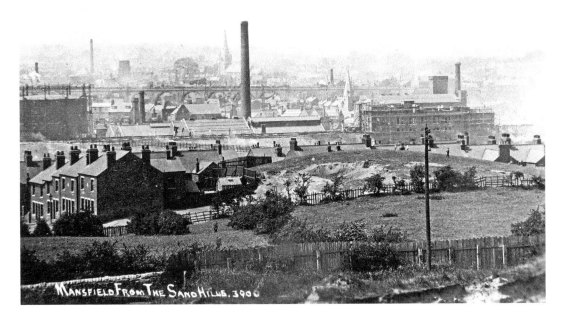

Town with a View

With the exception of the iconic 1875 railway viaduct traversing the town, together with the steeples of St Peter's and St Paul's to the right, and St John's on the left, the late Victorian vista of the town, as seen from Windsor Road, has changed a great deal. Gone are the polluting smoke stacks, mill, gasometer ... and the haze. In the clear twenty-first-century air, large trees now screen many of the viaduct arches. The concrete, multistorey Four Seasons carpark, and the curved, red-brick police station, with its rooftop solar panels, provide a more contemporary profile. (*Above*: Courtesy of Mansfield Museum)

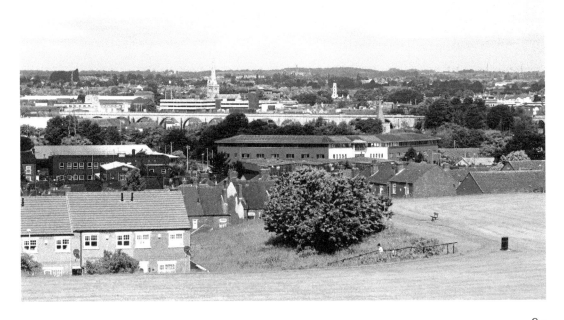

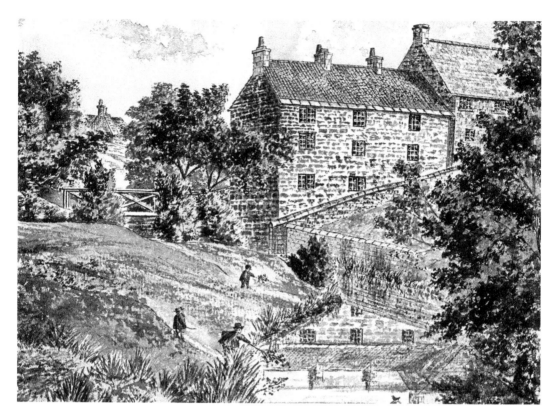

A River Runs Through

This idyllic 1866 watercolour by Joseph Seddon-Tyrer of the River Maun near Mansfield shows a river that has, since 1086, had its course almost completely manipulated by demands for power along its journey through the region. Rising to the north of Kirkby-in-Ashfield, the Maun makes its way north-east through Mansfield, with factories such as King's Mill, Hermitage Mill and Town Mill harnessing the river for power to drive the spinning mills. The Maun is dammed in several places. Such reservoirs and millponds are now converted tranquil gems of nature reserves and places of recreation. (*Above*: Courtesy of Nottinghamshire County Council, www.picturethepast.org.uk)

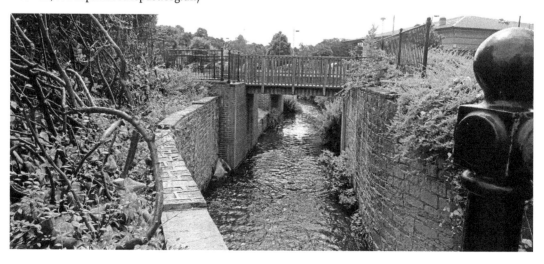

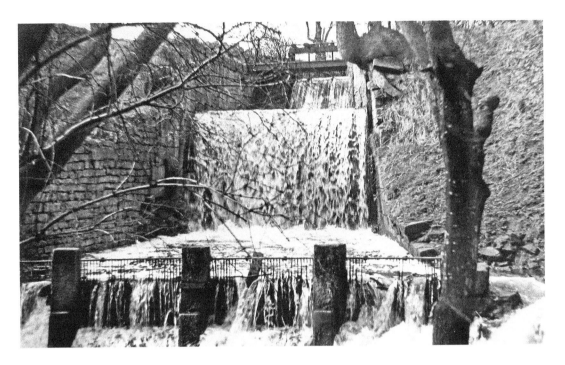

Driving the Wheels of Progress

A stepped, rustic, stone channel directs a cascade of water from a dam on the Maun, the site of Unwin and Heygate's Hermitage spinning mill. A series of millponds and reservoirs contained the river so as to supply a constant flow to turn the large waterwheels. Since the demise of the mills, the barrages remain. Today, Josias Jessop's King's Mill Viaduct, built in 1817 for the Mansfield and Pinxton Railway, provides an historical platform from which to watch the reservoir overflow zig-zag down a series of man-made steps, before dog-legging under the bridge on its way to another dam downstream. (*Above*: Courtesy of Mansfield Museum)

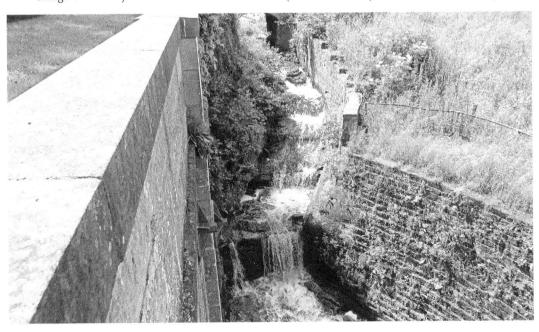

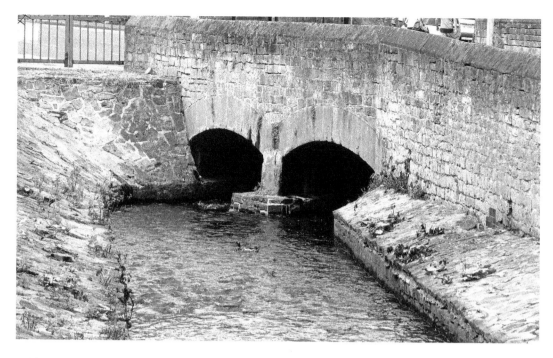

Bridge over the River Maun

Passing largely unnoticed under Bath Street, and flowing between the former brewery and the Army Reserve Centre, the River Maun flows through the twin arches of a low stone bridge on Littleworth. Originally built in 1820 (etched above the arches), the bridge was rebuilt in 1905. Much further upstream, a modern concourse and narrow bridge cross the King's Mill Reservoir barricade (*shown below*). The bridge takes pedestrians over the Maun and on to the Oakham Local Nature Reserve trail which, staying close to the river, brings the hiker to the Field Mill pond on Quarry Lane.

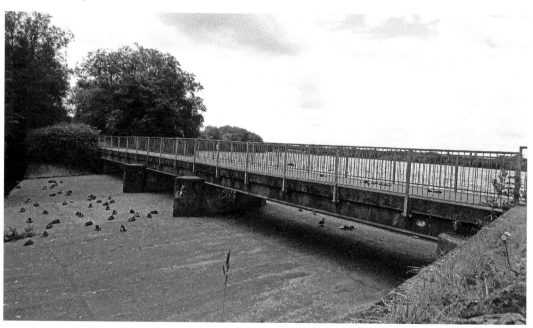

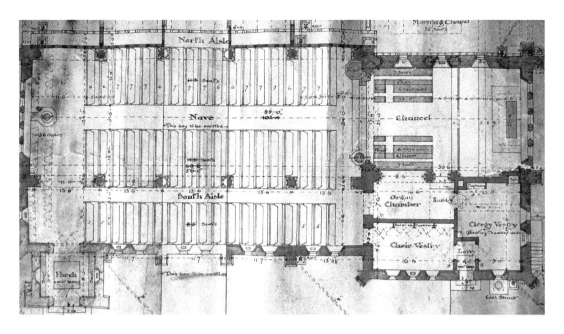

St Alban's, Forest Town

Consecrated in 1911, St Alban the Martyr Church was designed by Louis Ambler, but the north aisle was only added in 1937. The proposed chapel was never built however. The Anglican church was built on Clipstone Road in response to a need from the growing coal-mining community. As evidenced by the Commonwealth War Graves Commission's First World War graves, St Alban's was the spiritual home of many of the soldiers from nearby tented and hutted cantonments. The Duke of Portland donated the land and a grant of £2,000, while the Bolsover Colliery Co. contributed £600 towards building costs.

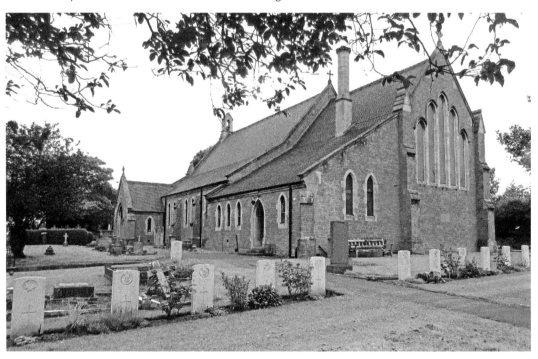

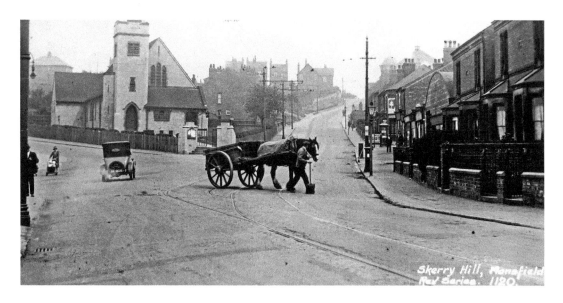

Church of St Lawrence the Martyr

Wedged between Skerry and Pecks Hills sits the Gothic-style parish church which dates back to 1909. In this early 1900s scene, a coal horse and cart crosses tramlines ascending Skerry Hill, while a smoke-belching automobile makes its way past the square, south-west church tower, with its stepped coping and rather unusual corner stack, rising above the main entrance. The Union flag flies over the site where all that has changed is the reduction in height of the front stone walls. Even the ornate wrought-iron arch carrying a light has endured. (*Above*: Courtesy of Mansfield Museum)

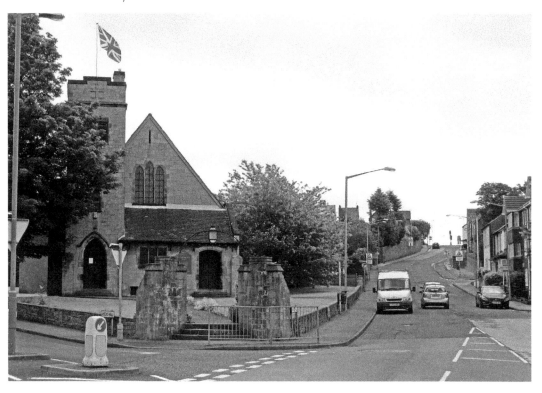

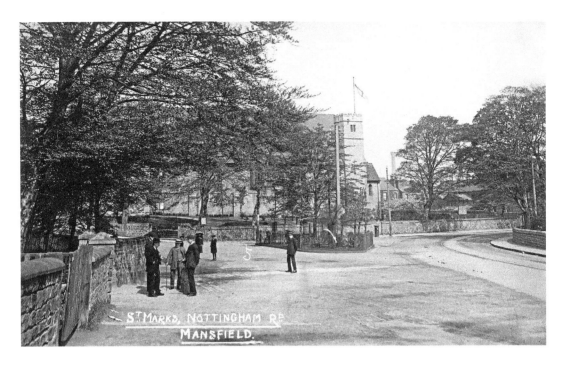

St Mark's

St Mark's Parish Church, the work of London-based architect Temple Moore, was built in 1896–97 at the junction of Portland Street and Nottingham Road. Constructed in a Perpendicular Revival style, the south-eastern tower has a crenelated parapet. In 1907, the two east windows were replaced with stained glass; the central window includes fragments of medieval glass. St Mark's vicar from 1894, the fifty-one-year-old Revd Arthur Gladstone Henley, tragically drowned in the sea while on holiday in Devon on 5 August 1904. The dual carriageway, Portland Street, can certainly no longer accommodate social gatherings of Edwardian gentlemen in their Sunday finery, sporting a miscellany of bowler hats, cloth caps and straw bashers. (*Above*: Courtesy of Mansfield Museum)

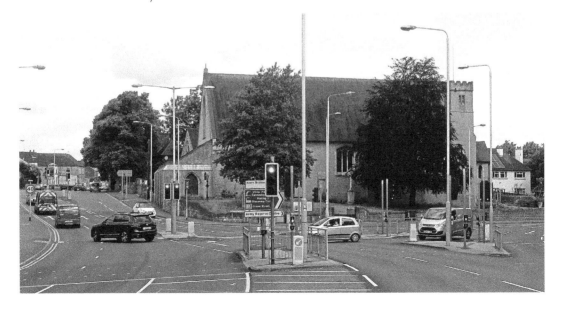

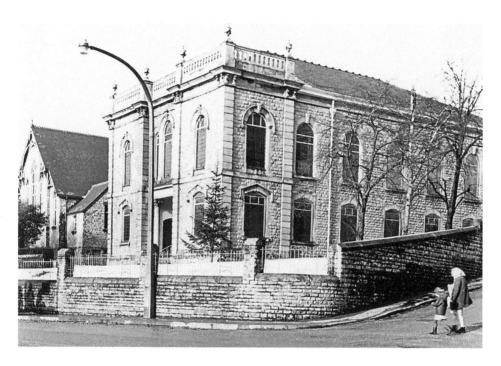

Bridge Street Methodist Church

Completed in 1864, the Italianate style, slate-roofed imposing church on Bridge Street has its origins in the late eighteenth century. John Adams, a Wesleyan preacher from Nottingham, first conducted services in 1788 by the water pump on West Gate. A church grew from these humble beginnings and eventually found a permanent home on its present site, replacing Stanhope House which once stood there. The Bridge Street flagship building today serves as one of several Methodist churches in the Mansfield and surrounding North Nottinghamshire area, appropriately referred to as the Sherwood Forest Circuit by the church. (*Above*: Courtesy of Mansfield Museum)

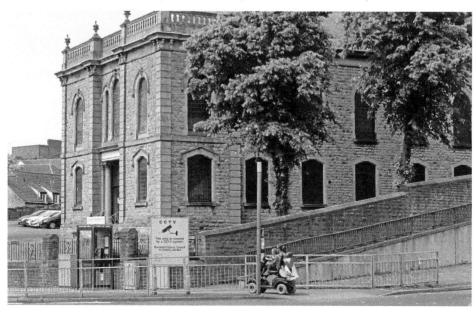

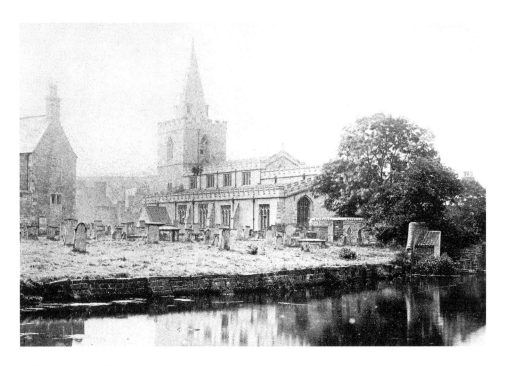

St Peter and St Paul's

A still River Maun millpond reflects the twelfth–fourteenth-century west tower of Mansfield's ancient Parish Church of St Peter and St Paul in this 1898 almanac photo. The seventeenth-century spire was restored in 1897. At a church bazaar held in the town hall in October 1888, reference was made to Mansfield Anglican parishioners numbering 13,637 at the time of the 1881 census, of whom 7,928 belonged to St Peter's and 5,708 formed into the 'ecclesiastical parish of St John's'. The graveyard has since been grassed over, and a parking area paved at the side of the adjacent St Peter's Centre, where rooms are available to rent for social activities. (*Above*: Courtesy of Mansfield Museum)

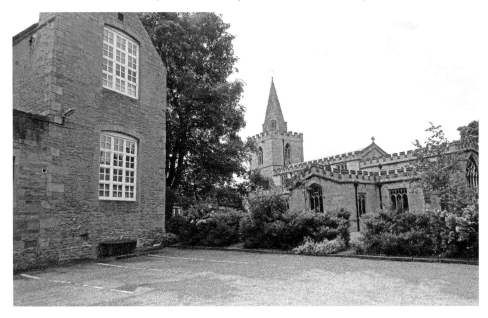

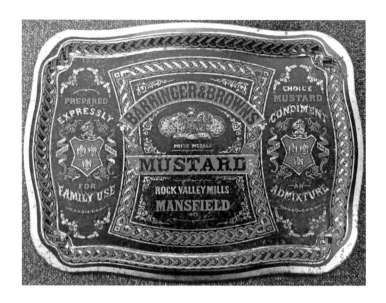

Of Mustard and Beer

A highly ornate tray, also manufactured at the Barringer, Wallis & Manners mustard mill, boasts of quality mustard from its Rock Valley Mills in Mansfield. In May 1879, the firm forwarded exhibits of mustard to the Sydney Exhibition to be held in September of that year. In the 1920s, at a time when the firm was manufacturing a wide range of commemorative biscuit and tea tins, it produced its first brewery tray, relying on orders from the Mansfield Brewery Co. to allow for the necessary capital investment in machinery for the double-action pressing process. A strong partnership ensued, with Metal Box waiter trays for many years serving Mansfield's finest ales. (*Above*: By the author, from the Mansfield Museum collection)

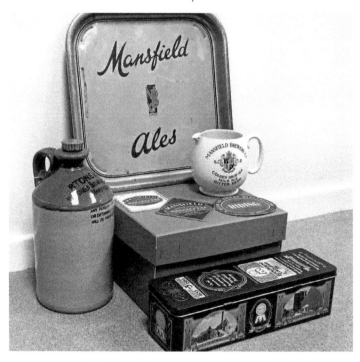

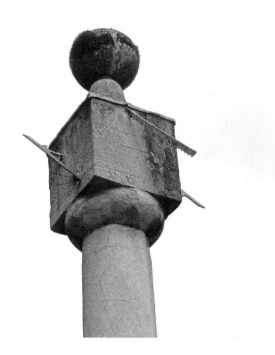

Mansfield Through Time

The *c.* 1600, Grade II-listed Old Market Cross in West Gate is officially described as a 'slightly tapered round shaft, topped with a cubical sundial with brass gnomons [the parts that cast shadows] and ball finial'. Although weathered, the Roman numerals are still discernible, a style that is emulated 400 years later and diagonally opposite, on the glass-covered clock face on the current BHS building. The times, however, have also caught up with this icon of the British high street, threatened with imminent closure at the time this book was written.

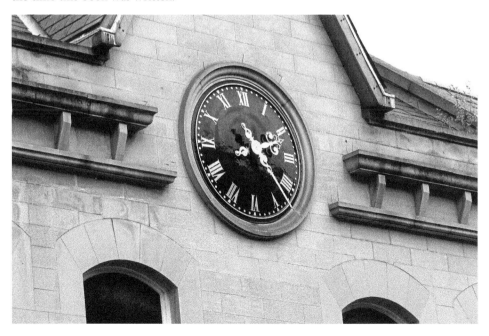

About the Author

Born and raised in Southern Rhodesia, full-time historian, researcher, copy-editor and published author Gerry van Tonder came to Britain in 1999, settling in Derby, the city of his wife Tracey's birth.

In Rhodesia he completed eighteen months' national conscription during the guerrilla war of the 1970s, before reading for a Bachelor of Administration (Honours) degree at the University of Rhodesia. He served as a Liaison and Returning Officer during the Zimbabwe elections, working through the period of transition from the ceasefire and return insurgents to assembly points.

Gerry has co-authored *Rhodesian Combined Forces Roll of Honour 1966–1981*, the landmark definitive *Rhodesia Regiment 1899–1981* (a copy of this book was presented to the regiment's former colonel-in-chief, Her Majesty the Queen) and authored *Rhodesian Native Regiment/Rhodesian African Rifles Book of Remembrance*. He has his own website: http://www.rhodesiansoldier.com He has just completed the co-authored *North of the Red Line: Recollections of the Border War by Members of the SADF and SWATF 1966–1989*, released in July 2016. He is also working on a further Rhodesian title, *Operation Lighthouse*, which is an account of the role of a para-military government ministry in the 1970s guerrilla insurgency.

This is Gerry's third book for Amberley Publishing, following *Derby in 50 Buildings* and *Chesterfield's Military Heritage*, released in April and July 2016 respectively.

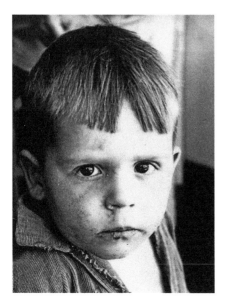 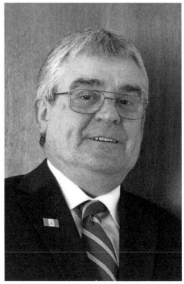

The author through time: 1960 and 2015.